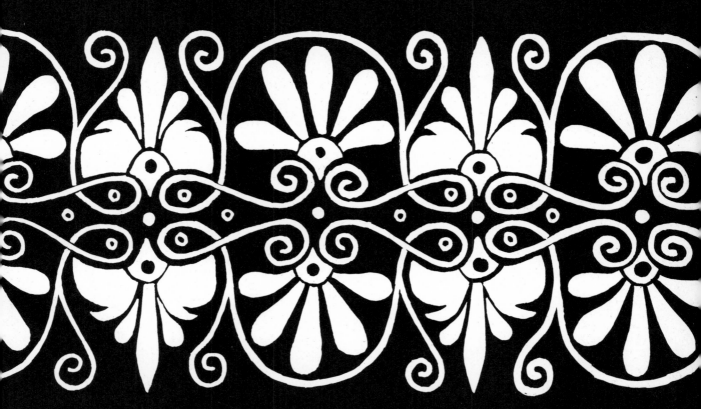

MEN OF ATHENS

MEN OF ATHENS

THE STORY OF FIFTH CENTURY ATHENS

REX WARNER

WITH PHOTOGRAPHS BY DIMITRIOS HARISSIADIS

BODLEY HEAD
LONDON · SYDNEY · TORONTO

© George Rainbird Limited 1972

This book was designed and produced
by George Rainbird Limited
Marble Arch House
44 Edgware Road, London W2
for The Bodley Head Limited
9 Bow Street, London WC2

ISBN 0 370 01391 3

House Editor: Mark Amory
Designer: Gwyn Lewis
Maps by Edward Purcell
Index by Vicki Robinson

Photoset by
BAS Printers Limited
Wallop, Hampshire
Printed and bound by
Amilcare Pizzi SpA,
Milan

TO THE MEMORY OF SIR MAURICE BOWRA

SCHOLAR TEACHER AND FRIEND

ACKNOWLEDGMENTS

I must express my grateful acknowledgements to Penguin Books for quotations from my translation of *Thucydides: the Peloponnesian War*. I am also deeply grateful to the late Sir Maurice Bowra for allowing me to quote some passages from books of his which are mentioned in the text. REX WARNER

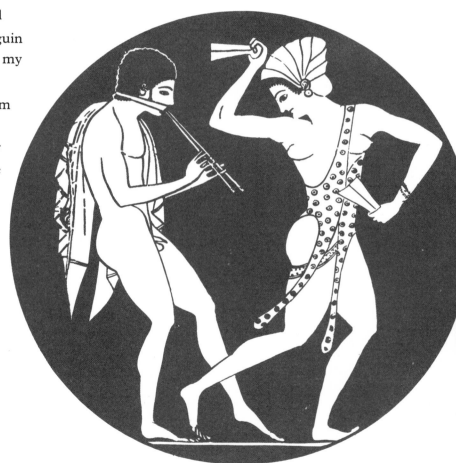

CONTENTS

Acknowledgments   6

List of Colour Plates   9

Map of Classical Greece   11

The Fifth Century   13

Aeschylus: The Old and the New   25

Aeschylus: Freedom and Authority   47

Pericles: The Power and the Glory   71

The Great Aim   89

The Building of the Parthenon   109

Sophocles   133

Sophocles: His Last Play   151

Euripides and Insecurity   171

Thucydides: Law and Nature   199

Aristophanes: War and Peace   219

Socrates: The End and the Beginning   235

A Short Book List   253

List of Illustrations and Acknowledgments   255

Index   261

LIST OF COLOUR PLATES

Women at fountains, from
a vase   *page* 17

Kore   18

Painting of a hoplite   27

Frieze with youths setting
a cat and dog   28–9

Frieze with gods fighting giants   30

Bronze head of a warrior   39

The Mycenaean walls on
the Acropolis   40

Marble horse   57

The Blond Boy   58

Zeus holding a thunderbolt   67

The Areopagus   68–9

Pericles   70

Remains of the Long Walls   79

The Treasure House at Delphi   80

Apollo   97

Woman in profile   98

The Parthenon   115

Artemis, from the Parthenon
frieze   116

Boys carrying water, from
the Parthenon frieze   *page* 125

Caryatids from the
Erectheum porch   126–7

Poseidon   128

The Varvakion Athena   137

The Strangford Shield   138

Painted knucklebone   147

Temple of Poseidon at
Sounium   148–9

Delphi   150

Departing warrior, from a
vase   159

Charioteer   160

Dionysus, from a vase   185

The abduction of Basile
by Echelos   186–7

Dionysian scene, from a vase   188

Temple of Athena Nike   197

Theatre of Dionysus   198

Nike loosening her sandal   215

Woman seated on a tomb,
from a lekythos   216

CLASSICAL GREECE

THE FIFTH CENTURY

I suppose that it would be true to say that the following beliefs have been and are generally held about the fifth century B.C. in Athens: it was one of the greatest, if not the greatest, period in the whole history of mankind; in this brief time not only were the basic principles of nearly all our arts, sciences, philosophy and politics either discovered or for the first time clearly defined, but in many cases the actual achievements – for instance in architecture, sculpture, tragedy, comedy and political democracy – reached a kind of perfection that has never been surpassed. True, not all of these achievements can be regarded as wholly Athenian and not all of them can be neatly packed into the boundaries of a single century. By the time of Pericles the great age of the epic was long past; there were philosophers in Ionia and in Sicily long before Anaxagoras came to Athens; the Parthenon was the finest and most splendidly decorated building in Greece, but it was not unique. Yet it remains true that in Athens and during what is known as the age of Pericles there did occur a sudden and most brilliant concentration of all the power, vigour, grace, daring and versatility which we associate with the highest and most advanced civilisation. And especially we note, at least for very much of the period, a quite extraordinarily optimistic faith, apparently widely held, in the powers of man to understand and to control his environment.

One element in this splendid confidence is its conscious modernity. 'An Athenian is always an innovator'[1], say the hostile Corinthian envoys at Sparta – and the word 'innovator' could equally well be translated as 'revolutionary'. Pericles himself praises his own Athens for the same quality. 'Let me say that our system of government does not copy the institutions of our neighbours. It is more the case of our being a model to others than of our imitating anyone else.'[2]

And so, with very much evidence to support our view, we seem to see a picture of the Great Age of Athens as something altogether splendid, original and dynamic, something which came into existence suddenly and almost miraculously, the first age in history when man became fully conscious of his powers and fully used them, an

[1]Thuc. I, 70   [2]Thuc. II, 37

Before the fifth century Greek sculpture tended to be remote or hostile. This snake, remarkable for its animation, was vividly painted.

age pre-eminently of liberation, when not only did the Greeks, under Athenian leadership, free themselves from the domination of the alien culture of the East, but when the human spirit finally broke free from the chains of superstition and of fear.

It should be added that neither the Corinthian envoys, nor Pericles himself, nor anyone else imagined that such a state of affairs could possibly exist without continued struggle and unremitting efforts. To Pericles this was as it should be and his words are eloquent:

> What I would prefer is that you should fix your eyes every day on the greatness of Athens as she really is, and should fall in love with her. When you realize her greatness, then reflect that what made her great was men with a spirit of adventure, men who knew their duty, men who were ashamed to fall below a certain standard.[1]

The Corinthians, while agreeing with Pericles that this is in fact the way the Athenians do live, take a less kindly view of all this strenuous endeavour: 'Their view of a holiday is to do what needs doing; they prefer hardship and activity to peace and quiet. In a word they are by nature incapable of either living a quiet life themselves or of allowing anyone else to do so.'[2]

Now these words of the Corinthians may suggest to us that our imaginary picture of the confident revolutionary dynamism of the Athenians, with all its splendid and liberating achievement, does not tell the whole story. And we should be warned, if by nothing else, by the structure of the Greek language itself of the extreme difficulty, or impossibility, of making any statement about the Greeks, and particularly about the Athenians, which will exclude an opposite statement or, at least, a modification. The Greek language is uniquely equipped to take back with one hand what it proposes with the other. In sentence after sentence we find clauses introduced by those words which we awkwardly translate as 'On the one hand . . . yet on the other . . .' Then there are the numerous methods of introducing antitheses: 'in theory . . . in fact', 'according to justice . . . according to nature', and a hundred others.

[1]Thuc. II, 43   [2]Thuc. I, 70

These three torsoes join below the waist to become a twisted bundle of serpents, perhaps Proteus, a sea-god.

OPPOSITE: *The Acropolis, a great rock to the south of Athens, bears remains of temples and walls from pre-Greek and sixth-century days. Cimon built the great walls early in the fifth century and the main buildings were erected under the direction of Pericles after 450.*

The language itself, then, will lead us to conclude that Greek thought is exercised within a consciousness of contradiction, stress and tension. When we say, rightly, that the Greeks 'saw life steadily' we must remember that what they saw so steadily was a vast and conflicting variety and when we say that they 'saw it whole' we must remember that though they certainly sought for a unifying principle, this principle was never a dogma; it always included multitudes. The nearest we get to dogma is in such statements as 'Strife is Justice' or 'The way up and the way down is the same way', simplifications which are in themselves recognitions and reconciliations of opposites.

That harmony was the aim, often attained, of the greatest thinkers, artists and writers of the age is certain; but it is a harmony that comes from tension and contains conflicts and motion which, if suspended in a kind of timelessness, a classic calm, are still present, still active, still alive. There is indeed the sense of rule and of measure, but there is nothing mechanical or diagrammatic about the rule. Most people who look for the first time at the Parthenon in Athens are struck by the fact that it is somehow unlike what they had expected to see. They came to see a building, but what they see is more than a building. It is a building which adds to itself, while keeping at a distance, the varied ring of mountains and the sea. It seems to have sprung in a perfection of art from the natural rock of the Acropolis, like Athena from the head of Zeus, a most uncommon and indeed miraculous birth, yet somehow natural, almost inevitable, tranquil in its self-assertion and vivid in its calm. Man's conquest of the material of marble is complete, but it is not abrupt or forceful. In this apparently rectilinear building there are no straight lines.

The Parthenon was one of the last great works supervised by Pericles himself and it may be thought of as a monument to his ideal of the perfect city, a city in which every citizen should be free and liberal, able to think and act for himself, but in which at the same time each should work for all and all for each, a city powerful enough to carry to all quarters of the Greek world its message of liberation, a city which, in its democratic organisation, had solved the contradictions of past history – the war of classes, unreasonable prejudice, blind self-interest and the rest – a city where Athenian man was at last free to develop all the finest human qualities and to lead others in the same direction.

It was a splendid ideal and, as Pericles had prophesied, it was to be an inspiration to others for the rest of history. Yet, with all our wonder at and admiration for the so-called Golden Age, we must remember that, except in memory, in art and in retrospect, the gold did not last, that the pursuit of this earthly paradise ended in disaster, that the chosen and disciplined freedom which Pericles had sought passed through a process of indiscipline and self-seeking to a lack of confidence, a failure of nerve, a willing acquiescence in what, to Pericles, would appear as despotism.

Below the Acropolis in Athens one may see, in the Byzantine churches, examples of an architecture much later than the Parthenon, but still ancient. These buildings look inward rather than outward; they restrict rather than welcome space, light and air. The soaring columns have gone and their place is taken by arches and domes;

In the fifth century Greek women had no education, no property and no vote; they did not attend parties, except in a professional capacity, and were not expected to walk out alone. But they were not the objects of contempt that has been assumed; within the limits of private life it seems likely that they were respected and, on occasion loved. Here they can gossip as they fetch water.

the illumination is not that of the sun but that of lamps reflected from metal. The images to be worshipped or revered are utterly unlike those designed or made by Phidias, who, like Pericles, made his gods Athenians and his Athenians gods. They are creations of a wholly different faith and outlook on life, an outlook which accepts and almost rejoices in mystery, a faith not in Man but in God.

The Greek Empire of Byzantium had a history of more than a thousand years and a power enormously greater than that exercised by Athens for less than a century. Her achievements in architecture, administration, scholarship, theology and much else are superb. By many of the standards most often used for measuring success – wealth, power, organisation, self-sufficiency, duration – this Byzantine civilisation may be considered as one of the most successful that has ever existed. Many patriotic Greeks today, when thinking of the greatness of their tradition, will think first of the Golden Empire of Constantinople, the second and the greater Rome, and only later, if at all, of the so much smaller city of Athens, with its brief history as a sovereign power, whose political ambitions, however expansive, can be seen to have ended quite quickly in failure, disorder and subjugation.

Certainly we must agree that the long and splendid history of Byzantium provides us with the most striking evidence of the tenacity, brilliance and versatility of the Greek spirit. Evidence of these same qualities can be found also in the conquests of Alexander and in the history, again a long one, of the Hellenistic successor states. And we must deplore the fact that, until comparatively recent years, the history of the greatness both of Byzantium and of the Hellenistic kingdoms has been neglected in the education of the West. Many schoolboys used to be, and perhaps still are encouraged to believe that after the death of Alexander, and perhaps even after the death of Pericles, the Greeks suddenly and rather unaccountably became 'degenerate'. Some of the responsibility for the prevalence of this ignorant and prejudiced attitude is often, and rather unfairly, laid at the doors of Gibbon.

It is true that Gibbon regards his history[1] as the history of a decline, but in its course he constantly pays tribute to the vigour and resilience of the Greek spirit in the long struggle against apparently impossible odds. However, although he abundantly gives honour where honour is due, he certainly finds something in the long and splendid history which indicates either a falling off from or a loss of a great good. While he can point to many great lawyers, architects, artists, generals, scholars and administrators, there are no great poets, no independent thinkers outside the realm of theology, which was in itself limited. In the great age of the Renaissance in Western Europe after the conquest of Constantinople by the Turks, the age which was to be the beginning of modern Europe and America, no single Greek, with the exception of one solitary painter (El Greco), was to play an important part. What the exiled scholars of Byzantium had to offer to the West was the relics of a distant past carefully preserved and throughout it all still alive. Through these men of the Middle Ages became innovators, rediscovering their lost youth and, in a sense, a lost maturity.

Gibbon himself ostensibly dates his 'decline' from the age of the Antonines, but,

[1] *The Decline and Fall of the Roman Empire*, Edward Gibbon. London, 1776–87

A kore or maiden in the traditional pose but losing the archaic stiffness and elaborately, affectionately decorated.

like the historian Tacitus, who lived under the Antonines, he is aware, and frequently reminds us, that there was a decline which started much earlier. Again like Tacitus he looks back, perhaps rather sentimentally, to the lost liberty of the early Roman Republic, but he is fully aware that it was Athens who gave that Republic her laws and gave to the world the principles of rational thought. One may reasonably suppose that Gibbon too would have accepted in outline the glowing picture of Periclean Athens which we gave earlier.

But he too would have recognised that the picture was incomplete. He would know that even in Pericles' own lifetime there were many of his fellow citizens who regarded his brilliant and daring policy as itself a 'decline' from the ideals of the recent past. Before the century was half over Athens, the nurse of freedom and the school of Hellas, had become in the eyes of many 'the tyrant city' and it was not long before the Spartans, of all people, were to represent themselves in the role of liberators. Pericles, by means of the Athenian art of political democracy, seems to have aimed at creating or fostering nothing less than a new type of human being. His fervent and truthful admirer Thucydides tells us, with a passionate sadness and indignation, of how the great experiment ended. Younger men, themselves thoroughly Athenian, seem to turn entirely against the world of their youth, which we think of as that golden age. Xenophon admires Sparta and even the Spartan sense of humour; he is careful to avoid offending Spartan susceptibilities and spends the happy years of his retirement in the Peloponnese. Plato, a much greater thinker and even more of an Athenian than Xenophon, considers that such statesmen as Themistocles and Pericles did much more harm than good and his contempt for 'the democratic man' is almost unbounded. His political ideal is still to be found in the city state, but his imagined Republic is very unlike the Athens which he knew and which Socrates loved. He had seen Socrates condemned to death by a restored democracy and his youth had been passed in a time of war and revolution. Even so ardent an admirer of Pericles as Thucydides had recognised that these conditions had led and, 'while human nature is what it is', always would lead to a general deterioration of character. But Pericles himself, in those few years of apparently unlimited hope, had trusted in this 'human nature' at least so far as the Athenians were concerned; he commended an almost boundless freedom which he believed would be not so much limited as reinforced by self-discipline and patriotism. Plato could not share in this confidence. His Republic aims indeed at a kind of freedom, but it is to be gained by an imposed discipline. Even Homer is to be expurgated.

In subsequent history lip-service has been given from time to time both to Plato's aristocratic ideal of the happy well-ordered state controlled by its philosopher-kings and to the total democracy of Pericles, in which every citizen was to have a voice in the administration of affairs and in the decisions of policy. But it must be admitted that no such state as Plato's Republic has ever existed at all and that, after the fourth century, the total democracy of Pericles has never existed again. Greek governments in Athens during the last half-century have censured Plato for his immorality and have either expurgated or suppressed the words of Pericles because of their dan-

One of the few surviving examples of religious images of its period. The taut deliberately archaic pose, combined with the fullness of body, the motion of arms and folds, and the serene head reveal the beginning of the new approach to a more human divinity. Probably Hera or Persephone, 480–470.

gerous revolutionary implications. It is a grave error to regard 'democracy' as something always or often characteristic of the Greeks. As has been well pointed out, while 'democracy' is a Greek word, so also are 'tyranny', 'monarchy', 'aristocracy', 'despotism', 'oligarchy' and 'plutocracy'. Today very large areas of the world are under the control of governments which call themselves 'democracies'. A Greek of the fifth century, if he were able to visit modern America, England, France, Russia or China would certainly be bewildered and might, with the inventiveness of his race, coin a new word or words to describe what he saw; otherwise he might select either 'tyranny', 'oligarchy', 'despotism' or 'plutocracy'. It needs little imagination to be sure that 'democracy' would not be the word to occur to him.

Yet today in our modern democracies we still find some who, like Pericles, look to the future with hope and confidence, others who, while conscious of the dangers and difficulties of the times, feel that with a little disciplinary rearrangement of forces things might yet go right, and still others who have already begun to despair and to wonder whether the whole history of the last 2000 years which, in all its variety, has been so largely based on the discoveries made by the ancient Greeks in a few centuries, has not been after all a colossal mistake. Is our belief in the validity of rational thought a misguided belief? Can any answer be given to any question? Has the individual any duties at all to the community, or the community to the individual? Is our faith that in the universe there is some principle of order or of justice a tenable belief?

Such questions as these are urgent and none the less so because they have always been asked, even though at some periods they have seemed less pressing than at others. They have never been asked with more urgency and with greater clarity than during the years of Athenian enterprise and discovery.

This is one of many reasons why the study of this period is not only fascinating in itself but is, above all, in the current phrase, relevant to our condition. It is much more than a study of our origins; it is a study not only of what we were, but of what we are or may become.

Though the answers given then to the radical questions which perplex us now are seldom precise, they may still be found valid and indeed at the present time particularly so. Certainly the questions are expressed with more candour, force and simplicity than is usually the case at the present day. Though it may seem that we seldom learn from the past, it is still possible to do so. And from this particular past it is possible to learn much so long as we can see and feel in it our present and our future.

In the following pages, which are concerned with the thought and action of a few individuals, much has, of necessity, had to be left out; for instance the economic factors of the time, the details of the elaborate structure of the democracy, military and naval tactics, and the place of slaves in society are all important subjects and none of them has been discussed here. But a further discussion of them, however desirable, would add little to the main argument of this book.

The late classical ideal of beauty, based on a fourth-century original, this head of Aphrodite shows how gods have become indistinguishable from idealized humans.

AESCHYLUS

THE OLD AND THE NEW

Among the many contrasting or contradictory elements which we notice everywhere in the life and thought of the Athenians – elements from which can come both harmony and disintegration – a most important one is the simultaneous consciousness of both the very old and the very new. The Athenians were the greatest of all innovators and were extremely proud of it; they were also extremely proud of their antiquity and of their traditions. They claimed to be among the very few people in Greece who had always lived in the same place on their own land. On their Acropolis were still the remains of the Cyclopean walls of the Mycenean age, whereas Mycenae itself was ruined and forgotten. It was men of their race who had crossed the sea to Ionia and there kept alive or recreated the Homeric epic. It would be possible to regard the Spartans and the Dorians in general as new arrivals on the scene. And by the time of Pericles it would also be possible to regard the Spartans as hopelessly out-of-date, limited in outlook, hide-bound by convention, unenterprising and lacking in that restless and practical intelligence which was the peculiar mark of the Athenian.

It is evident that throughout the fifth century the new Athenian and the old Athenian existed side by side and often in the same person. In Athens any question could be asked and any belief challenged, yet an event like the mutilation of the Hermae, when a number of time-honoured primitive statues standing at the entrance of houses were one night mysteriously defaced, could throw the whole city into a wild and superstitious panic. Pericles knew the physical causes of eclipses and was able, we are told, easily to calm down the crews of his ships who were afraid to sail when the sun was partially obscured. Yet not long afterwards and at the height of the period of intellectual enlightenment so sober and well-educated a general as Nicias lost his whole army because an eclipse of the moon inhibited him from action.

For most of the century there was always a pro-Spartan party in Athens and until Pericles came to power this party was usually dominant. What they admired in the Spartan way of life was a discipline and a sobriety which seemed lacking in Athens. At the beginning of the century they were far from averse to the Athenian expansion

By the fifth century the single combat between chieftains of Homeric days had given way to straightforward struggles between infantry, the only tactical device being the ambush. The military season was from March to October and the usual method of provoking opposition was to threaten or destroy enemy crops. This bronze helmet, normally adorned with a crest of dyed horsehair, afforded effective protection, but restricted both vision and hearing.

overseas in the process of liberating Greeks from the King of Persia. Indeed the most successful of Athenian commanders was Cimon who, while his ideal was a partnership in power between Sparta and Athens, in fact did more than anyone else to lay the basis for the later Athenian imperialism which became increasingly hostile to Sparta. It was only after Pericles took the place of Cimon as leader of the state that the pro-Spartan party began to complain of the new imperialism and to have serious doubts about the new democracy.

This party may be called and indeed often called itself the party of the aristocrats, 'the best men'. But the Greek word *aristoi* can be translated not only as 'best', but as 'the nobles' and sometimes as 'the rich'. And it should be remembered also that most of the first leaders of the new democracy came from the best and noblest families. The only exception, Themistocles, was indeed one of the greatest of all leaders, but in spite of having saved Greece at Salamis and having secured the future power of Athens in the negotiations following the Persian War, he was soon driven into exile by a combination of his enemies in Sparta and among the aristocrats in Athens. Paradoxically (except that so much in Athenian history is paradoxical) the statesman who was to carry out to the full the democratic and anti-Spartan policies of Themistocles was Pericles, a man who in every meaning of the word was an aristocrat.

His example and that of, amongst others, Aeschylus should be enough to show us that it is a mistake to consider a nostalgia for the past as something peculiarly aristocratic, or a faith in the present and the future as the distinctive mark of the democrat. The greatest men of the fifth century knew perfectly well that the past is often imagined as having been more splendid than it actually was and that the future, though predictable in some very general terms, must always be uncertain. But they knew also that in the past are to be found elements of permanent value and importance. The military tactics and logistics of the Trojan War were certainly almost childish in their simplicity and inefficiency; the heroic and tragic temper of the *Iliad* was still valid and would, unlike any political structure, last for ever. The spirit of the heroic, 'aristocratic' age speaks very frequently through the mouths of Aeschylus, Pericles, Sophocles and indeed Alcibiades. They too cling to the Homeric precept: 'Always to excel and to stand out ahead of the rest', a precept which, as Werner Jaeger has pointed out, was once a commonplace in European classrooms but which is now in many quarters distinctly suspect or flatly rejected. Nowadays such ambition can be frowned upon by a Christian moralist whose notion of humility it offends and even more often by those romantic or doctrinaire democrats who consider all distinction as obnoxious and pride themselves on, or struggle to attain, 'normalcy'. Such people existed also in ancient Athens and when they had an effect, it was usually disastrous.

But though the Homeric ideal still stood, its form was entirely different. The Homeric heroes are not political animals and the city state was something unknown to the epic. In the totally new political organisation of the city, the heroic qualities were recognised indeed as still valuable. Courage, strength, beauty, courtesy, rever-

Citizens who could not maintain horses, but could afford to equip themselves, served as hoplites. The core of the infantry, they were slow and heavy in attack, but could withstand the assaults of archers or cavalry. This one, from a painting, is called Megakles the Fair.

OVERLEAF: *Youths setting a dog against a cat. They sit with their fashionable staves, while the animals prepare to struggle. Dogs were popular pets, though there were also packs that roamed the streets, living off garbage.*

ence for the gods and the willing choice of death before dishonour were still to be admired, but these qualities had of necessity to be shown in conditions which were both wider and more restricted than those of the Homeric world. A Spartan or Athenian citizen army was something very different and militarily something far more effective than any force that Agamemnon could have put into the field. There might still be some class distinctions; the cavalry, for instance, or 'knights', came from the richer or nobler families; but the weight and strength of an army was in its disciplined heavy infantry, where each man depended on his neighbour and where the glory of victory or the shame of defeat was shared by one and all. This was something most unlike the amorphous mobs who do battle in the *Iliad* and whose advances and retreats depend entirely on the prowess of whatever individual hero on one side or the other is for the moment winning a personal glory. To the reader of the *Iliad* Achilles' refusal to fight because he has been insulted by Agamemnon seems perfectly right and proper; in the city state, as in any modern state, his conduct would be condemned as '*lipotaxia*', dereliction of duty, and would be punished as such. In the city state no natural or god-given superiority can raise any individual above the law. And the law is the reverse of what is despotic or oppressive. 'The people', says Heraclitus, 'must fight for its law as for its walls.' The main distinction between Greek and barbarian is that the Greeks have laws made by themselves and are therefore free, whereas the barbarians, governed by the arbitrary edicts of a king, must be, however admirable their personal qualities and however wise their monarch may happen to be, slaves.

In spite of the great differences between the two states, this general view would be accepted by Athens and Sparta alike. But these two states indicate clearly enough how variously the same principle can be applied. The Spartan system of rule by law, the *Eunomia* attributed to Lycurgus, was much older than the Athenian system. According to Thucydides[1] at the end of the Peloponnesian War Sparta had enjoyed the same constitution for four hundred years. The Athenian democracy at that time was scarcely one hundred years old, but in that short period had transformed the world of thought and action. Sparta, in the four hundred years of her *Eunomia*, had made no advances except in the military field. Under her system of law the citizens remained much as they always had been, except when they were (from the Spartan point of view unfortunately) exposed to foreign influences. In the Spartan system, as in the Athenian, there were contradictory tendencies, but in Sparta no one seemed aware of them, while in Athens everything was exposed to scrutiny and before the end of the century even the sacred principle of law itself came under attack. This principle was as sacred to Pericles as it had been to Heraclitus or indeed Lycurgus (though Pericles applied it very differently). Socrates, who lived throughout the century, reverenced the laws as deeply as had Pericles, but among his pupils and contemporaries there could be found some who regarded the laws as mere conventions, a device discovered by the weak to keep the naturally strong in order. To them tyranny or 'dictatorship', as we would call it, was not a word to excite fear

[1]Thuc. I, 18

The gods are fighting the giants, awesomely anonymous in their helmets. Apollo and Artemis shoot arrows and the defeat of the giants has begun—though armed and unhurt, one on the right is fleeing.

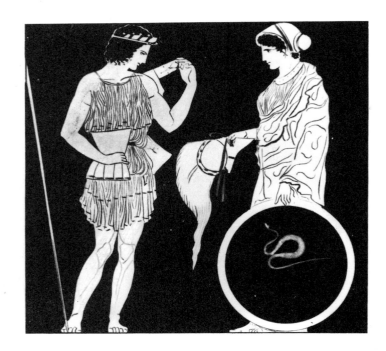

and loathing, but something desirable and, in fact, merely a restoration of the natural order of things. The gods and Justice, once accepted as universal principles and sanctions for the morality of the state, were themselves thought of as mere conventions.

At the very end of the fifth century, at a time when these ideas were already prevalent, when at the close of the long and disastrous war Athenian empire and the Athenian democracy were already staggering to collapse, Aristophanes wrote his greatest comedy, *The Frogs*. The main action of this play concerns the bringing up from the world of the dead a poet who can save the city in her hour of desperate need. The idea that at such a moment of crisis what was needed was, of all people, a poet would not have seemed to an Athenian audience a mad or merely comic notion, as it would to us. England can boast of as many poets as could Athens, but at the moment when England stood alone against Nazi Germany, if anyone had imagined the resurrection of a saviour from the past, the names of Drake, Marlborough or Wellington would have occurred long before the names of Shakespeare, Milton or Tennyson. But to the Greeks and especially to the Athenians, poets had always been acknowledged legislators and the poetry itself, though the themes were usually taken from a remote mythology, is always, in its particular way, contemporary and political. Another difference between then and now is the fact that the Athenian

FAR LEFT: *Marble gravestone of Aristion. He is seen wearing a bronze helmet, breastplate and greaves and holds a lance.* ABOVE: *Warrior putting on arms.* LEFT: *Achilles and Ajax, intent on a game presumably involving dice, as Achilles is saying 'tesara' (four) and Ajax 'tria' (three). Each, a great leader, has two spears and clothes and armour of elaborate elegance.*

LEFT AND FAR RIGHT : *Archers, one shoots, the other selects an arrow amongst five.* CENTRE : *The gods fighting rebellious giants. Athena (out of the picture) has clubbed a giant with her shield. Ares, the god of*

audience, coming from all classes, must have been thoroughly familiar with all the poetry of the time. Otherwise the wit, the humour and the seriousness of Aristophanes could not possibly have been effective, as we know they were. His imaginary literary contest takes place between the very vigorous ghosts of Euripides, the modern poet, and of Aeschylus, the poet who, while often considered as somewhat old-fashioned by the younger generation, was still admired and was, after all, one of those who fought at Marathon. In the end it is Aeschylus, the voice from the past, who is summoned up to earth 'to save the city' and to renew its greatness.

The choice is not surprising, for Aeschylus is pre-eminently the poet of the first spring of that confident and dynamic optimism which indeed had shaken the world. Not only had he fought at Marathon and Salamis; he had seen the overthrow of tyranny in Athens, the birth and startling successes of the new democracy and the beginnings and growth of an empire. One may imagine that he would have been more than a little annoyed at being considered old-fashioned. In fact he was both in art and in thought one of the greatest of the innovators. His theological speculations were at least as daring as those of Euripides; his treatment of the tragic themes, for all its grandeur, is strangely contemporary; in his play *The Persians* he brought

war, astride a fallen companion, raises his shield against the rock and lance of two giants. Hermes, also attacked by two giants, holds in his left hand the sheath of a short sword, presumably wielded in his right.

recent history on to the stage and in the *Oresteia* even the gods appear before an Athenian court of law.

But it is not for his modernity that he wins the prize in Aristophanes' play. It is because he represents the imagined stability of the glorious past, the days of the 'Marathon-fighters', the days when politicians were patriotic and honest, the simple, noble days in which it was possible to believe in something, when religion and morality were respected and not questioned and undermined from all sides by the pupils of those subversive characters, Socrates and Euripides.

In fact, of course, by this comic over-simplification Aristophanes was being grossly unfair to everyone concerned and no doubt he was aware of this himself. Socrates and Euripides were patriots just as Aeschylus was and like him they respected tradition. Many of their admirers however did not and certainly by the end of the century it was difficult for anyone to feel that there existed any longer an established way of thought and action which led unquestionably to health, happiness, justice and success. As usually happens at such times, there were many who, like Aristophanes, looked back nostalgically to a past in which life was simpler and more heroic and people were not yet vexed and troubled by the doubts and complications of the

present. The glorious days of the first half of the century may have seemed to fulfil these conditions and it was natural to regard Aeschylus as the poet and prophet of that splendid time. This point of view may be considered as aristocratic, but it was not so in any narrow sense. The leaders of the people in those times were certainly thought of as greater men and better leaders than those of later days, but they led a free people and were chosen for their qualities rather than for their wealth or families. The admired discipline was self-discipline, and not enforced.

And in fact there is much to be said for this view of Aristophanes, if indeed this was his view, although, as we shall see, the tensions of his own day, and particularly the tension between the new and the old, modernism and tradition, existed also in the days of Aeschylus.

Aeschylus, alone of the three dramatists, had lived near a period when there were tyrants in Athens. He was not born at the time when Pisistratus died in 527; but Hippias and the other sons of Pisistratus held power for another twenty years. Then the democracy was restored, or rather entirely reshaped, by Cleisthenes, a member, as was Pericles later, of the noble clan of the Alcmaeonidae. It was this new democracy which in 490 performed the apparently impossible achievement of defeating at Marathon a Persian expeditionary force which aimed at restoring power to the aged Hippias, who, if the expedition had been successful, would have ruled Athens with a mercenary army and made her, as much of eastern and northern Greece already was, subservient to Persia. Aeschylus certainly fought at Marathon and probably also at the much more decisive battle at Salamis ten years later. It is likely that he shared with his fellow countrymen a detestation for the whole idea of tyranny and joined with them in singing the popular drinking songs glorifying the 'tyrant-slayers', Harmodius and Aristogiton, who had killed Hipparchus, the brother of Hippias.

In the cool judgment of Thucydides this action was not so glorious as it had become in popular sentiment. 'The conspiracy of Harmodius and Aristogiton', he says, 'originated in the wounded feelings of a lover, and their reckless action resulted from a momentary failure of nerve.'[1] He considers that up to the time of the murder the tyrants had ruled moderately and in accordance with the existing laws, only making sure that one or other of them was always in office. In fact the age of the tyrants was far from being an age of reaction. As elsewhere in Greece, the tyrants depended for their power over the great nobles on the support of the common people and, in particular, of the new commercial and trading classes. In a sense it was the dictatorship which, by weakening the power of the old land-owning nobility, made the rise of the democracy possible. This was also the period of the beginning of Athenian expansion overseas and of the cultural transformation of Athens herself. The competition in tragic drama at the feast of the Dionysia was instituted in about 534. It was the tyrants who brought to Athens from Chios, now occupied by the Persians, the written text of the Homeric poems and organised their recitation as a part of the great festival of the Panathenaea. New and more splendid temples and

---

[1] Thuc. VI, 59. Hipparchus had attempted to seduce Harmodius, the friend of Aristogiton.

'The archaic smile' in this case enigmatic and lost in reflection

public buildings were put up and planned for the future, some of them on an enormous scale. Indeed the great temple of Olympian Zeus, planned by Pisistratus, was not finished till the time of the Emperor Hadrian.

The tyrants may be said to have ushered in the new age, but they were scarcely part of it. The Athens visible to Aeschylus in his youth was still, in many ways, archaic. The statues still had 'the archaic smile'; the buildings were primitive in comparison with what was to come later. Indeed Aeschylus died before the great buildings of the Periclean age – the Parthenon, the Propylaea, the Erectheum – had been either planned or constructed. The temples which he would remember from his boyhood and early youth had been destroyed in the invasion of Xerxes, as had been the ancient wooden walls of the Acropolis, behind which a few of the old and the conservative, in a mistaken interpretation of an oracle, had attempted to shelter. The future was to be secured by the new and genuine 'wooden walls' of a victorious fleet and by the new fortifications which, under the influence of Themistocles, had been in places hurriedly put together out of the fragments of the temples destroyed by the Persians.

But though Aeschylus did not live long enough to see the new buildings on the Acropolis which were to glorify and sanctify the power and splendour of Athens, he not only witnessed but in an important way helped to shape the cultural and political revolution which was as rapid as and much more lasting than the growth of Athenian power. The dramatic contests held at the spring festival of Dionysus had been inaugurated ten years before Aeschylus was born, but little or nothing is known of Aeschylus' predecessors in this new and entirely Athenian art. It is commonly believed that tragedy developed out of the dithyramb, a form made up of mimetic dances and of a song which narrated a story. Thespis is supposed to have been the first to change narration to a kind of drama by introducing one actor separate from the chorus, who was actually to impersonate the leading character in the story instead of merely telling the story as a narrative. It was Aeschylus who added a second actor and then later followed the example of Sophocles who increased the number to three. Each of the three actors was, of course, able to take more than one part, since at any one time the stage might be occupied entirely by the chorus or by only one or only two actors.

Of these changes far the most significant was the introduction of the second actor. This innovation made it possible to present the clash of wills and of ideas which are the essence of drama. A new art had been born which contained elements of both epic and lyric, but was in itself something entirely different. And in the hands of Aeschylus and his successors it was to be, of all forms of poetry, much the most representative of the fifth century.

In spite of enormous differences, this Athenian drama resembles in some important ways the drama of Shakespeare. Professor Kitto applies the term 'religious drama'[1] to both, and at first sight his choice of words may appear surprising. No god or gods appear on Shakespeare's stage, while in Aeschylus they are never far away and often

[1]*Form and Meaning in Drama*, H. D. F. Kitto. London, Methuen, 1956

Bronze head of a warrior, originally with a helmet. Found on the Acropolis

appear in person. In one play, the *Prometheus Bound*, all the characters are gods except for Io, and she is destined to bear a child to Zeus. Aeschylus also is very obviously attempting 'to justify the ways of God to Men', whereas Shakespeare rarely, if ever, ventures into theology. In his day there was an established church, a priesthood and a dogma – things which never existed in ancient Greece. Yet in Shakespeare's tragedies we notice the same concern for the meaning of life as we find in the Athenian dramatists, the same hopes and fears for an order which is surely founded and for a morality that can be welcomed and understood. He also lived in an age of rapid and increasing change and of extending horizons, of fascinating discovery and of bewildering doubt and schism, of pride and assurance in the new and of reverence for a traditional past. In the defeat of the Spanish Armada England also had known the triumph of a Salamis. In England also the individual was beginning to take a new place in society and, although democracy was not then and is not now anything like as complete as it was in Athens, there was already the same urgent debate and canvassing of the claims of rights and duties, of freedom and authority. It was already asked again whether man or God was 'the measure'. If 'the world's great age' was inaugurated in Athens, it began anew in the Renaissance under conditions which, with all their differences, are very similar in important respects.

The huge stage of Shakespeare with its procession of kings and queens, statesmen and generals, lords and attendant lords, mobs and mob-leaders, soldiers and artisans, certainly seems at first sight to be something utterly different from a Greek drama in which most of the action is between two or three characters, much of the time is taken up in choric singing and dancing, and scenes of violence only very rarely take place on stage. We may notice, however, several points in common. Both Shakespeare and the Athenian dramatists set their plays in the more or less distant past; the protagonists are not only in themselves somehow larger than life, but are also, by their titles or their position, given still further trappings of grandeur; their language too is, as a rule, raised above the common level. And yet, though the characters may be as far separated in historical time from the contemporary audience as were, for example, Agamemnon or Coriolanus, the feeling, thought and action of these characters was and still is entirely contemporary. Emotions which have always been felt by all men everywhere are engaged in both cases and they seem to be more fully and perfectly expressed in a language, a style and a setting which, in spite of being often, in a modern sense, unrealistic, have the effect of putting in a clearer and more piercing light what is always before the eye, but is seldom so well seen.

The very important aspect of the new individualism which appeared both in fifth-century Athens and in Elizabethan England is the conflict between the revolutionary spirit and authority. The doctrine that to the strong all things are lawful is found in both periods. Some of the romantic attractions of such a view are expressed in Marlowe's *Tamburlaine* and in his analysis of political power Machiavelli often comes close to Thucydides. And in both Athenian and Shakespearian tragedy the hero, the man with exceptional gifts and exceptional force of character, plays a much

Remains of the Mycenaean walls before the Parthenon.

greater part than in the drama of any other period. But both Shakespeare and the Athenians insist that the hero, for all his greatness and, indeed, often because of it, is certain to be ruined unless he can come to terms with powers that are greater even than he is and may be described as God, or the gods, or, in another sense, as the divine order in the state, the city, the realm or the community.

It is in this very wide sense that Shakespearian and Athenian drama can both be called religious and also, in an equally wide sense, political. This does not, of course, mean that the chief concern of the dramatist was to expound any particular article of faith or develop any particular political theory. The dramatist's first consideration must always be to write a good and entertaining play. But both in Athens and in Elizabethan England the audiences seem to have welcomed or demanded for their entertainment a vivid representation of the conflicting and disturbing ideas of the time and a consideration of values and general principles. It is no doubt wrong to think of Aeschylus or Shakespeare as theologians and moralists rather than play-wrights; but it is much more wrong to neglect this aspect of their art and to think of them merely as contrivers of theatrical effects.

These dramas are both life-like and larger than life; they are set at a distance from us in time and space and language, but this is the kind of distance which serves to magnify rather than to diminish, and when this particular focus is changed in the direction of a common realism, as it is in the dramatists after Shakespeare and even in some of the later plays of Euripides, a completely different kind of drama is on the way in. In Athens there are no new tragedians after the death of Euripides and the old comedy disappeared at the same time. Writers and audiences became more interested in manners, in situations of ordinary life or in more or less abnormal psychological states than in the serious considerations of the extent and limitation of the powers of man or of society. And if ever attempts are made, as by Seneca and by Dryden, to recapture something of the grand and spacious manner of the great periods, the result is something melodramatic, sentimental or both. The writing, for all its rhetorical skill, is neither serious nor urgent.

Of course, while there are great and important similarities between Athenian and Elizabethan tragedy, there are also enormous differences and there are great differences too among the Athenian tragedians themselves, close as they are to each other in time. Time, however, in those days moved with such extraordinary rapidity that even a few years could make considerable differences in experience. Aeschylus was the only one of the three who died before the outbreak of the war which was to ruin Athens and Sparta alike. He was also the only one of the three who had seen Athens before the triumph of democracy. And this accident of birth may partially account for the fact that Aeschylus, profoundly conscious as he is of the dangers and horrors which are part of the human condition, seems to take a more optimistic view of history and of mankind than does either Sophocles or Euripides. Most of the tragedies, though not all, of Sophocles and Euripides are 'tragedies' in the modern sense and end in the death and ruin of the principal character or characters. They are also complete plays and are written with no idea of continuity with the two other

Odysseus giving Achilles' son his father's armour

plays which would be put on during the same day's performance at the dramatic festivals. Aeschylus, on the other hand, so far as we can judge from what remains of his work, preferred to work in trilogies. Within the trilogy each single play can certainly stand on its own, but it is still part of an interconnected design. Each of the first two plays, it seems, ends on a note of expectation, with a problem unsolved or only partially solved. But the last play will provide a solution in which the ways of God are justified to men and often particularly to the men of Athens. Indeed in the *Oresteia*, and possibly in the *Prometheia* also, Athens is the scene and Athenians are the human agents through whom the progressive movement of divine justice is made manifest. It is an evolutionary progress in time, leading from the worse to the better and working through the reconciliation of apparently irreconcilable opposites. Only one of Aeschylus' trilogies, the *Oresteia*, survives as a whole. The action here covers two generations and the general theme invites us to look both backwards and forwards in time to periods before the birth of Agamemnon and after the life of Orestes. The time-span covered by the *Prometheia*, of which only the first play, the *Prometheus Bound,* survives, is very much greater.

In the single self-contained plays of the other two tragedians the action often, though not always, takes place in a day or in a few hours, and the concentration both of action and of language has a tremendous effect. And there is something of the same concentration in single plays of Aeschylus, in the *Agamemnon*, for instance, or in the *Prometheus Bound*. Yet there is an important difference. At the end of Sophocles' *King Oedipus,* we are not inclined to ask, 'And what happened next?'. But at the end of Aeschylus' *Agamemnon* or *Libation-bearers*, although in the one play the action of Clytemnestra and in the other that of Orestes seems to be complete, we know that there must be more to come. Three separate plays, each capable of standing on its own, are all parts of a design which is not fully unfolded until the end of the last play.

J. H. Finley, in his admirable study of Aeschylus, writes, 'Aeschylus' main title may not be as the creator of tragedy but as the inventor of the idea of meaningful time.'[1] And what to him gives time its meaning deserves further consideration. Unlike Homer and Hesiod he does not regard the past, legendary or not, as having been greater or happier than the present. He sees clearly the conflicts, disabilities and savageries of the past, yet he sees also its greatness and its interconnectedness with the present. He exalts innovation and change, particularly as exemplified in Athens, but he finds only anarchy and dissolution in a change that cuts its ties with tradition. Both freedom and authority are necessities in his evolutionary process. Each may be presented as unyielding and yet each must yield to the other.

[1]*Pindar and Aeschylus*, p. 181, J. H. Finley. Harvard University Press.

A hoplite apparently at the moment of collapse

AESCHYLUS

FREEDOM AND AUTHORITY

Of the trilogy of plays which Aeschylus wrote on the theme of Prometheus, only the first play survives in its entirety and the fragmentary text and information which we have of the other two plays only provide scanty evidence of the complete working out of the theme. But what we do know for certain is that somehow or other in the end the utterly opposed powers of Zeus – the new dictator, the oppressor of the old gods, and of mankind – and Prometheus – the saviour and lover of mankind, the resistance leader *par excellence* – do in fact become reconciled.

Many romantics are and have been extremely shocked at the idea that Aeschylus could have allowed this to happen, and no one was more shocked than Shelley. In the preface to his own *Prometheus Unbound* Shelley writes, 'In truth, I was averse from a catastrophe so feeble as that of reconciling the Champion with the Oppressor of mankind.' But we know enough of Aeschylus to know that his catastrophes are never feeble and that, indeed, no adjective could be less appropriate for him. If 'feeble' means 'incapable or unwilling to face the full force and difficulty of facts', then it is Shelley, in his naïve and simple 'free thought', rather than Aeschylus, with his awareness of the necessity of tension, who deserves the epithet. Indeed the catastrophe of Shelley's play is very feeble indeed. It is simply a lyrical vision of the millennium in which, somehow or other, Man and Nature are one, Freedom, Love, Humanity – all as understood by Shelley – have, somehow or other, triumphed over Oppression, Hate, Bigotry and the rest, and all tyrants and priests have disappeared. Mrs Shelley, in her *Note on Prometheus Bound*, does indeed speak of 'the mystic meanings scattered throughout the poem', but she admits that 'they elude the ordinary reader'.

The Greeks also employ abstractions, but these, unlike those of Shelley, are related to life as men live it. Yet we cannot dismiss Shelley's objection to the idea of a final reconciliation between Prometheus and Zeus simply because his own *Prometheus Unbound* is dramatically unconvincing. It is perfectly true that at the end of the first play in Aeschylus' trilogy our sympathies are entirely on the side of Prometheus. Yet by the end of the trilogy, though we do not know how so unlikely a result was

Agamemnon, commander-in-chief of the Greek forces against Troy. He married Clytemnestra, whom Aeschylus makes a formidable figure in contrast to her feeble though blustering lover, Aegisthus; so that when they conspired to murder Agamemnon, the responsibility was hers.

Orestes, an infant when his father was killed, was ordered by Apollo to avenge the murder; this meant committing the dread crime of matricide. This he did (above left), killing the lover first, before turning on his mother.

contrived, the audience must have been induced to think well not only of Prometheus but of Zeus also. Some critics have attempted to meet the difficulty by suggesting that in Aeschylus' view gods as well as men evolve, that just as men change from savagery to civilisation, so does God change from bad to good. They point out that such a view is utterly at variance with all Judaic or Christian ideas about God, but often omit to mention that it is almost equally at variance with Greek views on the subject. Some support for the theory can certainly be found in Greek mythology, which is much more varied and ambivalent than Hebrew doctrine. In Homer the gods do behave very much like men, except that their power is greater and that they can have no fear of death. Their power, however, unlike that of the Hebrew or Christian gods, is not unlimited. Even Zeus cannot save his favourite, Hector, or his son, Sarpedon, who are fated to die, and, though Zeus is certainly supreme on Olympus, he is apt to justify his supremacy by the crude statement that he happens to be stronger than all the rest put together. In fact there is never any change in the divine nature. Gods do not, like men, learn by suffering; they cannot learn because they cannot suffer. The only exception to this rule – and it is an important one – is that, according to the myths, the divine hierarchy can certainly be changed by

The Erinyes, avengers of evil, especially that committed against relatives, pursued Orestes and here frighten the oracle at Delphi, where he had taken refuge.

revolution, the revolution of the sons against the father. Kronos castrated Ouranos and was in turn overthrown by his son, Zeus, who himself was challenged by the Giants and had to fight hard in order to consolidate his supreme power.

These old stories, shocking as they are to a moralist (and no one was more shocked than Plato), are the background of the *Prometheus* and are made use of also in the *Agamemnon*, where the chorus of old men seem to imply that these unfortunate things may have taken place long ago but that now there is only one supreme god, Zeus, and that his rule, however difficult it may be to understand, is based not only on Power but also on Justice. However, as the trilogy of the *Oresteia* develops, we discover that this power is still far from being unchallenged. There are still in the dreadful Erinyes powerful representatives of the older gods. They not only dispute, but flatly deny the right of Zeus's delegate, Apollo, to execute justice by instructing Orestes to avenge his father's murder by killing his mother. And in the end their claims are acknowledged to have great force. The jury of Athenians, sitting for the first time in the Court of the Areopagus, having heard both Apollo and the Erinyes state their cases, give equal votes for each side, and Orestes is saved only by the casting vote of Athena herself. Even then the Erinyes are very reluctant to accept the verdict. Finally it is not by force, but by persuasion, that Athena finds a solution to a problem which, like that of the *Prometheia*, seems quite insoluble. The Erinyes are to retain their powers and to be honoured where before they were feared or loathed. But these powers are to be exercised under a new dispensation. Crime is still crime and must be punished, but the punishment will be under a new rule, the rule of enlightened law, the law of Zeus, which regards not only the act itself but all the circumstances leading up to the act. And so the old gods, the terrible Erinyes, really do change their characters and become instead the Eumenides, the Kindly Ones, who have their permanent home in Athens.

The conclusion of the *Oresteia*, then, certainly seems to support the view of those who maintain that Aeschylus made use of the myths in an evolutionary manner, so that, dramatically at least, the divine beings who appear in his plays are indeed capable of progressive change. Whether this was what, as we say, Aeschylus 'really believed' is an entirely different question and one that cannot possibly be answered. He might, no doubt, be supposed to have believed that, while the divine nature does not change, it is increasingly revealed to man in the process of the evolution of society; on the other hand, it is just as likely that he never gave this metaphysical problem a thought. It is well to remember that he lived at a time when, for better or for worse, there were no theologians and no literary critics.

There was, however, an extraordinarily keen interest and much theorising about politics and, in a very wide sense, justice. And, though the plays of Aeschylus certainly raise moral and metaphysical problems, it seems likely that both the poet himself and his audience would be more concerned with the political than with the religious implications of the themes. Not that, in any case, they were inclined to separate the two. It was known, or dimly remembered, that for centuries human society had been in a state of conflict and, if there ever had been a Golden Age, it was so remote as to be almost meaningless. What was certain was that here, in their own city and in recent years, a change had taken place and was still going on. The internal conflicts of the past seemed to have been settled, or almost settled; and this had come about not by the violent assertion of one interest over others, but by a just reconciliation of conflicting interests which had ended in a confident unity and in a strength that had proved able to resist and overcome the Persians, the greatest power on earth. The sign of the despot and of the tyrant was an inability to feel the force of Persuasion; the strength and promise of the new democracy lay in the fact that Persuasion was honoured and that, after reasoned debate, the best solution was found and voluntarily followed.

Certainly Aeschylus, and no doubt many others of his fellow citizens, knew that this was not always the way things went; that a corrupt speaker could often outdo an honest one in the art of persuasion; that a democracy could be as greedy and as unjust as any tyrant. But these facts had not yet become apparent to all Athenians just as even now they are not apparent to all citizens of the diffused and much watered down democracies of our own days. To those who, like Aeschylus, had fought at Marathon and had seen the city of Athens rise triumphant from the Persian

The decision whether Orestes is guilty is hard to make, but Athena, uniquely qualified as a disinterested judge as she herself sprang motherless from the head of Zeus (opposite), absolves him.

invasion, the achievements and the promise of the new system were clearly evident and, while admitting the dangers and uncertainties of all human affairs, they must have felt pride in the present and hope for the future.

This pride and hope shine through the closing passages of the *Oresteia* and it has been reasonably conjectured (though there can be no certainty here) that the conclusion of the *Prometheia* may also have been a joyful one in which the old gods, represented by Prometheus, and the new gods, represented by Zeus, are reconciled, with the scene of reconciliation again set in Athens. However this may be, there certainly was this reconciliation which Shelley found so shocking.

Shelley's feeling was in many ways natural and even, though he would not like it said, conventional. It reflects a kind of millenarian outlook which has been shared by many people who are not, as Shelley was, professed atheists and rebels. This outlook is older than Christianity but has been particularly prevalent under Christian influence. It is an outlook of which we find scarcely any trace in fifth-century Athens, where such phrases as 'the Kingdom of Heaven on earth', 'the Rule of the Saints' or 'of the Free Spirit', 'the withering away of the State', would have been either unintelligible or repulsive. The man without a city was thought of as the most unfortunate of all creatures and, though within the state there were frequent, indeed almost constant, divergencies and oppositions, these were all set within a framework which in itself was recognised as being good and necessary. The great political crime was *pleonexia*, grasping at more than one's proper share or taking more than one ought to have. It was this that was characteristic of the tyrant and justified his assassination, and even a suspicion that one man was becoming too powerful was often enough to lead to ostracism, a limited period of exile. The crime was common enough and was disapproved of on moral as well as on political grounds. But no one would dream of imagining that the state organisation itself, which among other things enforced, where necessary, obedience to the laws, could be anything but good. The idea that the pure spirit, liberated and enlightened, could be so far above the state as not to be subject to its regulations would have seemed the idea of a madman; and the Marxist theory that all forms of state government are necessarily instruments for the suppression of one class by another would have seemed equally absurd.

Political feelings certainly ran high and political hatreds were bitter. It was normal and natural to hate one's enemies and to love one's friends. But enemies were hated simply for the harm they had done or were capable of doing; it was still possible to find some sort of accommodation by which enemies could become friends and the desired state of harmony, under which all interests could be satisfied and safeguarded, might come into existence. The Greeks had plenty of experience of the horrors of war and revolution, but they were spared the horrors of religious wars. They did not kill or enslave each other for the sake of God nor think that people of a different race or religious beliefs somehow deserved to be exterminated.

The oppositions between Good and Evil, between this world and the next, between God and Caesar or between the Flesh and the Spirit, were not felt to be so absolute and compelling as they came to be regarded in later centuries. The figures of the martyr and of the rebel were, on the whole, looked upon with distaste rather than admiration. It is most unlikely that even so great and so sympathetic a figure as Aeschylus' Prometheus would have excited in an Athenian audience quite such unmixed approbation as he did in Shelley and has done in many others. A modern audience can scarcely help seeing in Prometheus a symbol of the unjustly oppressed who will in the end rise up and overcome the oppressor; indeed the importance of the myth in modern times rests almost entirely on this view of the righteous and defiant rebel or martyr, who is prepared to undergo any torture rather than recant or yield and who in the end will lead mankind into a happier and freer state. He is, in fact, Good in confrontation with Evil and it is assumed that Good or History is on his side.

It is certain that Aeschylus did not see things like this. If he had, he would have agreed with Shelley and refused to allow the possibility of any compromise between the Champion and the Oppressor of mankind. It will be helpful to examine briefly what in fact we see and hear in the play. We may find that it is not precisely what we expected to see or what we thought that we were seeing.

The play opens with four figures on the stage. There are the Titan Prometheus, the new god Hephaestus, who is a son of Zeus, and the two abstract figures of Power and Violence, who are servants of Zeus. They are there to see to it that Hephaestus carries out the orders of Zeus, which are, as Power tells us at once,

> to discipline and pin down
> this outlaw here upon the lofty ragged rocks
> in the unbreakable bonds of adamantine chains.

This, we are told, is to be his punishment for stealing fire and giving it to man.

In the dialogue between Power and Hephaestus which follows, Power speaks throughout with great brutality, urging Hephaestus to the work and taunting Prometheus on his suffering. Hephaestus acts with the greatest unwillingness. He is sorry for Prometheus, whom he regards as a kinsman and a fellow god, and insists that it is only under compulsion that he is doing what he has to do.

All this time Prometheus has not uttered a word. It is one of those scenes, apparently common in Aeschylus (Euripides makes fun of them in Aristophanes' *Frogs*) where the main character makes a great effect by silence and immobility. It is only when the stage is empty that, in a soliloquy, he laments his fate, calling upon the powers of nature:

> O heavenly air, and breezes swift upon the wing,
> fountains of rivers and innumerable laughter
> of the waves of the sea, and earth, mother of all,
> and you, all-seeing circle of the sun, I call,
> see what I suffer, a god at the hands of gods.

He knows the future, 'all of it exactly', as his name (Forethought) implies, but he knows too that it is impossible to fight against Necessity. He is aware that his suffer-ings have come simply because of his gift of fire, that civilising force, to men.

The chorus now enters. It consists of the daughters of Oceanus, another of 'the old gods', but one who has made his peace with Zeus. In a short lyrical passage Prometheus again indicates the misery of his condition and the chorus express their sorrow and compassion for him. They point to the fact that:

> New rulers now hold power on Olympus

and they assure Prometheus that all the gods are sorry for him:

> All are indignant at your wrongs,
> all except Zeus, and he,
> ever angry, with a mind set,
> never bending, crushes down the sons
> of Ouranos, nor will he cease before he sates his heart,
> or by some force another steals his empire hard to win.

Prometheus retorts that a time will come when 'the president of the immortals' will indeed need his help against this very eventuality. He alone knows a secret on which the power of Zeus depends and, unless he reveals it, in the end Zeus is bound to fall from power; but he will never divulge it until Zeus is willing not only to free him but 'to pay recompense'. The language reminds one more of Achilles in his anger against Agamemnon for wounding his honour than of a Christian martyr, and it is to be noted that Prometheus has said nothing at all about injustice. The chorus gently reprove him for his unyielding attitude; he is 'speaking too freely', they tell him: Zeus's mind will never alter.

Prometheus replies that he knows the character of Zeus and gives him that of the typical tyrant by saying that he 'measures what is just by his own interests'; never-theless he will be broken down in time and will be anxious enough to claim peace and alliance with Prometheus.

The dialogue now changes into the more pedestrian iambic metre and Prometheus, in reply to a question, explains how the quarrel with Zeus arose. His explanation is extremely interesting and is cast almost entirely in terms of contemporary politics. It all began, he said, when the gods split up into different parties, and the word he uses is '*stasis*', the word invariably used to describe the political factions of the time. Some of the gods were in favour of deposing Cronos in favour of his son Zeus; others were equally eager to prevent Zeus from ever seizing power.

Prometheus himself had the advantage of the advice of his mother, Themis, and of Gaea, the Earth, who are apparently the same person ('one shape [person?] of many names'). She constantly

> had foretold what was the future dispensation –
> that the way of fate was not by strength or force of might:
> victory and power proceeded from intelligence.

Prometheus had attempted to explain this to his Titan brothers, but they had refused to listen to him. He had therefore taken his mother with him and joined the party of Zeus and Zeus had been glad to have him on his side. It was owing to the plans of Prometheus that Zeus had been victorious and had been able to hurl down Kronos and his party into Tartaros. But after this Zeus turned against his benefactor. Prometheus comments:

> This is a sickness, it seems, that goes along with dictatorship – inability to trust one's friends.

and the word translated 'dictatorship' is, of course, '*tyrannis*', 'tyranny'.

The reason for the quarrel was simply that Zeus, after his victory, wanted to do

Satyrs lighting their torches from the fire stolen by Prometheus in a long fennel stalk

away with mankind and create another race instead. The rest of the gods approved, but Prometheus did not. Instead he raised mankind from its abject condition and set it on the path of civilisation. It was this act that led to his present suffering.

Up to now, it seems, the chorus, or at least some members of the chorus, have been somehow suspended in the air and speaking from some kind of magic chariot. Now, at Prometheus' request, they come down to earth, but the machinery which brought them is almost immediately in use again as Oceanus, another of the old gods, who was, presumably, either neutral or in the party of Prometheus and Zeus during the war in heaven, appears on a winged horse.

Oceanus is genuinely anxious to help his friend and kinsman and offers his services as a mediator between Prometheus and Zeus. He feels sure that, if only Prometheus will curb his language a little and show some signs of submission, Zeus can be won over. But Prometheus rejects the offer. He recoils from the idea of appearing before Zeus as a suppliant and in any case regards any such mission as that proposed by Oceanus, as futile; Zeus would never listen. And so, after some debate, Oceanus goes off again on his 'four-foot flyer'.

The character of Oceanus is certainly not heroic and it is easy to think of the scene as a kind of 'temptation' in which Prometheus is encouraged to give in weakly to injustice instead of standing up firmly for his beliefs. But it is very doubtful whether an Athenian audience, or Aeschylus himself, would have seen it quite like this. Oceanus, while not heroic, is not a mere time-server; he is genuinely sorry for Prometheus and the points he makes are good ones. When he says:

> This point, Prometheus, you must recognise – that words
> can act like medicine for a spirit in distress,

the audience would approve the sentiment, and they would admit also the truth of Prometheus' reply:

> Yes, if one soothes the heart when the heart is ripe for it,
> not if one represses by force a bursting anger.

But, true as this may be, this way of feeling is not necessarily admirable.

After Oceanus has gone the chorus sing an ode expressing the 'cry of mourning' that has been raised by mankind and all nature because of the suffering of Prometheus and his brothers. They comment:

> Here Zeus unhappily
> rules by the laws he made himself,
> to the gods of old revealing
> arrogant tyranny.

Next, Prometheus describes in detail his work of giving civilization to man. In this imaginary account of man's primitive state there is no hint at all of any Golden Age. On the contrary men were at first helpless and ignorant creatures, living in burrows and incapable of ordered thought. The steps by which Prometheus led them to civilisation were these: first he taught them to observe the rising and setting of stars and constellations and so to mark out the seasons; then came the art of using numbers, 'that master science', and the arrangement of letters which implied 'a discursive memory' and so became 'mother of muses'. Next came the domestication of animals and the art of ship-building. And there were other arts and sciences which he revealed, the greatest of which was the art of medicine; there was also the art of prophecy and of divination and the discovery of metals. He concludes:

> In this short word learn all the story together:
> Prometheus gave all arts and sciences to men.

In all this Aeschylus is writing from a rationalistic and modern point of view. Mankind is developing forward from a state of savagery rather than declining from an imagined state of happiness. Many of the old myths are passed over or rejected, such as the story of how Prometheus cheated the gods of their sacrifice by instructing men to burn the less appetising parts of animals to the gods and to keep the best

From the beginning of history there were two species of horse—the lazy, vicious European strain and the superior Arab. This impatient mettlesome creature must be the latter, as surely were those for whose owners Xenophon wrote two volumes 'On Horsemanship'.

bits for themselves. He is throughout a liberator and a benefactor, like the half-legendary Lycurgus of Sparta or, in recent times, the Athenian Solon.

The chorus admire him for what he has done and venture to hope that in the end he himself will be freed and 'hold a power no less than Zeus'.

Prometheus replies that a long time must elapse and much pain and suffering must be undergone before this happens. As he says,

> Science is weaker a long way than necessity.

The chorus ask:

> Whose hand is it that holds the tiller of necessity?

And his answer is:

> The threefold Fates and the remembering Erinyes.

It is an answer which recalls not only the passages in Homer which show Zeus unable to save the lives of his son Sarpedon and his favourite Hector, who are fated to die, but the passage in the Ionian philosopher Heraclitus, who tells us that if the Sun oversteps his measures, 'the Erinyes, the handmaids of Justice, will bring him back'. And it is not only possible, but likely, that the philosopher, if it were assumed that Zeus himself had overstepped the measure, would insist that he also would be brought back.

The chorus at once ask Prometheus:

> Is Zeus then weaker than the Fates and Erinyes?

And Prometheus replies:

> He will not run away from what Fate has in store.

How this will come about he refuses to say, though later in the play he does in fact tell them.

In the ode which follows the chorus again express their sympathy with Prometheus but do not entirely approve of his attitude. They imply that it is much safer, and probably wiser, always to revere the gods instead of, like Prometheus, 'following the way of a private judgment'. They seem to have forgotten that it was only by doing just this that Prometheus achieved his great work of civilising man.

Next occurs the episode of Io. She is somehow represented as being both a girl and a cow, though how this was done we have no means of knowing. To begin with she speaks wildly, as Cassandra does in the *Agamemnon*; she has been driven from land to land by the stinging gad-fly sent after her by Zeus's wife, Hera. Like Prometheus, she is an object of pity and her sufferings, like his, have been caused by Zeus. Prometheus immediately knows her and knows also her future history, which

---

The Blond Boy has almost entirely lost the deep yellow on his hair that gave him his name. His heavy, serious air is tinged with melancholy.

he is prepared to tell her, though the story will not be pleasant for her to hear. But
first Io herself tells the chorus of how it all began. Night after night she had been
visited by dreams in which she was urged to go out from her home to her father's
meadows and cattle-herds. She was told that she had been fortunate enough to be
chosen as the wife of Zeus himself. She told her father Inachos of this and he sent
to enquire the will of the gods from the oracles at Delphi and Dodona. After a number
of bewildering replies there finally came a clear answer, which was that Inachus must
turn her out of her house and land at once; if he failed to do so, Zeus would send
a thunderbolt to wipe out all his race. Inachus, 'against his will and mine', as she says,
obeyed the order. Immediately Io's shape was changed; she grew horns and was
driven madly onwards by the gad-fly. She was also watched and spurred on by Argos,
'the earth-born cattle-man' with his many eyes. Argos, in the end, was killed, but
Io was still driven on and on by the gad-fly.

The chorus are full of sympathy, but Prometheus checks them. So far, he says,
they have scarcely heard even the beginning of the sufferings which are in store for
Io, and in a long speech he relates what her wanderings will be from Europe to Asia.
The geography is somewhat confused, as it often is in the references in Elizabethan
drama to countries which are only vaguely, if at all, known to the English. But the
language is splendid and exciting. Prometheus breaks off to ask:

> Now, do you not think
> that the dictator of the gods with all alike
> deals violently? This mortal girl here he, a god,
> craved for his love and laid these wanderings on her.

At this point Io wishes that she were dead and asks herself why she has not long ago
destroyed herself. Prometheus reminds her that he himself has not even this remedy,
since he is immortal. His sufferings must last until the day comes when Zeus will
fall from his dictatorship. Io admits that she, like Prometheus, would be glad to see
this happen, but asks whether such a thing is possible, and Prometheus replies that
it is not only possible but certain, if Zeus is left to his own devices. He will in the
end marry a wife who will bear a son greater than his father. Zeus cannot possibly
escape this fate unless Prometheus is set free. And in reply to Io's questions he tells
her that his deliverer will be one of her own descendants:

> Third in descent after ten generations more.

This is all that Prometheus will reveal, but the audience of course would know that
the destined deliverer will be Heracles, the son of Zeus by a mortal and one who, like
Io and Prometheus, will spend years in suffering. Also that the fateful bride who is
destined to bear a son greater than her husband is Thetis who will be married not
to Zeus, but to a mortal, Peleus, and whose son will be Achilles.

Next Prometheus resumes his account of Io's future wanderings in Asia through
legendary peoples and monsters, the Gorgons, the griffins, the Arimaspians who live
by 'a stream rolling with gold'. These countries were soon to be described with

*With the gift of fire, Prometheus made possible all the joys of civilization, and so domesticity. Here a
woman places a folded garment in an unusual and elaborately decorated chest.*

The Greeks wrote in columns without gaps between the words, on perishable papyrus, but no manuscript before 425 survives. Here a woman (left) is intent on her reading while another (right) casually holds a torch.

greater accuracy by Herodotus. It was an age in which fabulous travellers' tales were rapidly turning into established fact, and it is easy to imagine the delight both of Aeschylus and his audience in descriptions which again remind one of those in Marlowe. From these far eastern districts Io will, somehow or other, arrive among the Ethiopians and will follow the Nile up to Egypt. There at last Zeus will give her back her wits again

> with just a touch and stroke of the hand that brings no fear.

This touch of hand will make her pregnant with her son, 'black Epaphos',[1] who will rule over Egypt. From him in the fifth generation will come a family of fifty women who will come back again to Io's own land of Argos as fugitives in order to escape marriage with their cousins. (This is a theme which Aeschylus had dealt with in his earliest surviving play, *The Suppliants*). Prometheus tells how, when the wedding is forced on them, all the girls will kill their husbands on the wedding night, except for one of them, who will choose

[1]Derived from a word meaning 'to touch lightly'

rather to be called irresolute than a murderess.

She will become the mother of a race of kings in Argos and from them, in the end, will be born the one who is destined to free Prometheus.

Now Io, again driven mad by the gad-fly, goes on her way and the chorus, in a short ode, describe the extreme danger in which any woman is placed if she is unlucky enough to be desired by any of the gods. They point out that:

> Far the best thing is to wed within one's station.

It is impossible to fight against Zeus.

Prometheus again assures them that the power of Zeus will not last for ever. Let him be confident now, sitting on his throne and brandishing his thunderbolts. This will not help him once he has equipped one far stronger than himself, one who will brush aside his thunderbolts. Then

> Zeus, stumbling on this misadventure, will find out
> how far apart are supreme power and slavery.

Now, in the final episode of the play, arrives Hermes, the messenger of Zeus, whom Prometheus contemptuously addresses as 'the lackey of the gods'. Hermes has come with Zeus's command that Prometheus must tell of this secret of the fatal marriage, which he claims to know, and, of course, Prometheus scornfully refuses. As he says,

> You and your powers are young, and so, no doubt, you think
> you dwell in towers where grief can never come. And yet
> have I not seen dictators twice hurled down from them?

He utterly refuses to make any concession at all. Let Zeus do what he likes. He can cause suffering but can never destroy Prometheus, who under no circumstances will ever ask mercy from an enemy.

Hermes describes in detail what will happen unless he changes his attitude. The whole of this place will be convulsed with thunder and lightning. For ages Prometheus will be buried under the earth and then, when he comes back to the light

> Zeus's winged hound, the blood-red eagle, greedily
> will tear into great rags the flesh of your body,
> coming, although not asked, to dinner every day.
> And he will feast upon and gnaw your liver black.
> And do not look for any end to pains like these,
> until a god appears to take upon himself
> your load of suffering, and is willing to go down
> to rayless Hades and the gloomy depths of Hell.

All this, he assures Prometheus, is no empty boasting. It is certain to happen.

> The mouth of Zeus does not know how to tell a lie.

Even the chorus now urge Prometheus to give in, but Prometheus is still defiant. Let Zeus do what he likes, he will never submit.

Hermes then advises the chorus to take themselves elsewhere and not be involved in the storm and earthquake which are coming. But the chorus prefer to suffer with Prometheus. They have learnt to hate all traitors and will stay with him to the last.

And so the play ends in thunder and lightning with Prometheus' final words:

> O my glorious mother, O Heaven
> with circle of light that is common to everyone,
> you see me and see this injustice.

As at the end of the first play in the trilogy of the *Oresteia*, a resolution of the antagonism has been reached which is definite enough for the time being but which is known to be only partial. Zeus has violently crushed his enemy and asserted his power, but we know that in the end nothing can save him unless Prometheus can be forced or persuaded to warn him in time of the marriage which will destroy him; and we know that Prometheus will never yield to force. If Prometheus keeps his secret, Zeus will beget a son who will be far stronger than he and who will violently overthrow him. There is no hint that this son will be in any way better or more just than Zeus; he will merely be stronger and so able to set up a new dictatorship or tyranny which, we may assume, is likely to be just as oppressive as the old one. And all this is far from being in accordance with what Themis has told Prometheus is to be 'the new dispensation', under which the future is to lie not with brute force but with intelligence. Now it looks as though this new dispensation is to be indefinitely postponed and there will be no change in the old and barren sequence of tyrannies succeeding tyrannies.

In just the same way the *Agamemnon* ends with the apparent triumph of one of the conflicting parties and with our foreboding that this triumph will only lead to more crime and greater injustice. Clytemnestra has avenged the death of her daughter, Iphigenia, and Aegisthus has settled his own family feud with the house of Atreus. But, as the play has emphasised from the beginning, all these crimes are part of a chain in which injustice has certainly led to punishment, but the punishment itself has been another act of injustice and a still greater crime. Clytemnestra may like to think of herself as an incarnation of the ancestral curse and as an instrument of justice. So was Agamemnon when he utterly destroyed Troy because of the sin of one man, Paris. And in a sense both he and she were in fact what they thought they were. Their mistake lay in assuming that such actions can possibly be final. And so, when Clytemnestra rather pathetically (if such a word can ever be used of her) prays for a truce with the ancestral curse and that the chain of violence and bloodshed may now be broken, we know – and indeed Cassandra has already told us – that she is praying for something quite impossible. Just as she killed her husband, so she in turn will be killed by her own son, and he, by this just action, will involve himself too in the apparently unbreakable chain.

If the problem of Orestes is set down in the following simple terms, there can be no possible solution to it: I A son must always kill his father's murderers. II A son must never kill his mother. III His mother has killed his father.

In the end a solution is found, but its difficulty is emphasised by the fact that the jury of Athenians cannot reach a clear decision between the claims of Apollo, who has instructed Orestes to avenge his father's murder by killing his mother, and the Erinyes, the older gods, who insist that nothing can justify matricide. Athena's casting vote which absolves Orestes is given for what appears the frivolous reason that she can vote in this way because she, personally, has never had a mother. In spite of this, however, she is, unlike Apollo, always courteous and polite to the Erinyes. She admits the general validity of their claims and promises them even more honour and security than before if they will consent to co-operate in a new and more civilised system of justice under which the old ancestral pieties are respected and safeguarded not by individual action but by the power and authority of a modern state which will seek the happiness and prosperity of all its citizens in a god-fearing and law-abiding community. And this community, an example to the rest, is, of course, Athens.

At the end of the *Prometheus Bound* we are also faced with a dilemma which appears insoluble. If neither Zeus nor Prometheus will change, there is nothing to look forward to except a perpetuation of injustice as one divine tyranny gives place violently to another. The only alternative is, as in the *Oresteia*, a new system altogether; and it is reasonable to suppose that it was along these lines that Aeschylus did find his solution. There was, at Colonus, near Athens, a cult of Prometheus Fire-bringer in which Prometheus was worshipped together with Athena and Hephaestus and it is tempting to imagine that, after his liberation and reconciliation with Zeus, Prometheus, like those other older gods, the Erinyes, was brought peaceably and honourably home to Athens, the city best suited to receive the great author of civilisation. But, attractive as such a supposition is, it must be admitted that it is supported by no concrete evidence.

What is certain is that a reconciliation did take place and it is impossible that this could have come about without concessions on both sides. That Prometheus should have made any kind of concession at all was, as we have seen, abhorrent to the absolutist mind of Shelley and to the minds of many other romantic revolutionaries. To a Greek it would be, under certain conditions, perfectly natural. No one was assumed always to have all the right on his side, nor was there anything disgraceful in accepting a proper reparation from an enemy for his injustice. Everyone would remember the great example of Achilles, who quite rightly refused to go into battle when he felt that he had been treated dishonourably, but who made a tragic mistake when he allowed his anger to carry him too far and to refuse the very reasonable peace offerings made by Agamemnon. Both in the poems of Homer and in the politics of fifth-century Athens, the words 'good' and 'evil' are not very forcible. The concepts of honour and dishonour are. And in the great minds of the fifth century these concepts are always present along with the more modern notions concerning national interest. The democratic leader, Pericles, shared with the aristocratic leader, Cimon, the keen sense of honour that inspires the actions of the *Iliad*. And Aeschylus felt as they did. Probably it was largely for this reason that he, rather than Euripides, was the poet summoned by Aristophanes to save the city in her hour of need.

Most of those who have discussed Aeschylus' treatment of the story of Prometheus have tended to look at it from some theological standpoint and have imagined that the poet was chiefly interested in such questions as the problem of evil and the difficulty of reconciling the fact of undeserved suffering with the existence of a just and beneficent deity. And these problems no doubt did occur to Aeschylus, though perhaps scarcely in those terms. But it seems likely that he was more deeply concerned with the political problems of his own time, the rapid change from one system to another, freedom and authority, the permanent value of the old and the promise and fascination of the new. With extraordinary dramatic force he stresses the opposition between the old gods and the new gods, but this is only in order to indicate finally the possibility of harmony. Both Prometheus and Zeus are real and are necessary just as in his ideal Athens the freedom and promise of the new democracy must rest on the authority and sanctity of an old tradition. We may regard the story of Prometheus as symbolic of the fact that in history, in manners, in morals, and in thought, progress can only take place by means of innovation (which must often be revolutionary), and yet continuous innovation will lead to insecurity and disruption, a state of affairs where 'the centre cannot hold'. There must come a point where consolidation is necessary, and yet no consolidation can be permanent except in a state of fossilisation. Prometheus needs his Zeus just as the democracy needs the aristocratic ideal; Zeus needs his Prometheus since without him he will degenerate into an inhuman tyrant.

One may imagine that Pericles would have sympathised with such a view, although it is impossible to say what Aeschylus thought of the speed and thoroughness of the innovations which Pericles made.

Zeus brandishing a thunderbolt

OVERLEAF: *The Areopagus, where the council of Athens met*

PERICLES

THE POWER AND THE GLORY

Pericles came from an aristocratic family and initiated the most far-reaching system of democracy that has ever existed. His mother was Agariste, the sister of Cleisthenes, the founder of democracy and a member of the great clan of the Alcmaeonidae. His father was Xanthippus, who had commanded the Athenian contingent of the allied fleet which had finally destroyed any hopes that the Persians might have had of a naval recovery at the battle of Mycale, off the coast of Asia Minor. This naval action was fought in the year after Themistocles, great victory at Salamis and was said to have taken place on the same day as the land battle of Plataea which resulted in the breaking of the Persian land forces and their withdrawal from Greece. Soon afterwards Xanthippus, with Aristides, was largely instrumental in the organisation of the Confederacy of Delos, which began as a voluntary league of Greek cities, under Athenian leadership, aimed at liberating those cities and islands which were still under Persian control and at assuring the independence of those that had already been freed. Up to this time the supreme command had always been held by a Spartan. That Sparta now willingly resigned the naval command and the continued prosecution of the war to Athens may be explained by the fact that the Spartan commanders on the spot were proving themselves recalcitrant to the home government and also, by their arrogant behaviour, making themselves increasingly unpopular with the allies. Sparta was naturally conservative and had always been reluctant to move outside her own boundaries unless she felt herself seriously threatened. She had, moreover, problems of her own at home where her large subject population was very often on the brink of revolt. So long as she was the dominant power on the mainland, she was quite content and it is likely that she was glad to see the Athenians expending their energies in campaigns far away from her own shores.

The Spartans did make one effort to check the growing power of Athens on the mainland. Soon after the end of the decisive campaigns against Xerxes and his generals they sent an embassy proposing that the fortifications of the Acropolis, which had been destroyed by the Persians, should not be rebuilt. The pretext was that, in the event of another Persian invasion, it would be advisable not to allow any

Pericles, the most influential man in Athens at the height of her achievement, wearing a helmet

fortified Greek city to fall into Persian hands. As for the Athenians, they would be welcome to retire behind the wall already built across the Isthmus of Corinth where they could fight a defensive action along with their Spartan allies. This pretext was clumsy enough. The real aim of Sparta was obviously to prevent the emergence of any Greek state capable of resisting pressure from herself. So long as a Spartan army could at any time occupy Athens, not even the Athenian fleet could for long challenge any demands that Sparta might make.

A group of old men deliberating, with Pericles himself on the left

The Athenians, of course, saw no prospect of another Persian invasion and were already, without the help of Sparta, making doubly sure that the Persians would never venture into Europe again. They had twice had their city burned and wished in future to be capable of defending it against all comers, the most likely of whom were certainly the Spartans themselves. At the same time they knew that at the present time, with their fortifications in ruins and their fleet with their best troops in the

Themistocles, champion of sea power

OVERLEAF: *Athenian power was based on her navy and so on the trireme. Each was about 120 feet long with a crew of perhaps 200 and a speed, assisted by sail, up to 5 knots. One aim in battle was to ram your opponent amidships.*

western Aegean, they lacked the power to resist, should the Spartans attempt to enforce their politely worded request. It was then that for the second time Themistocles secured the survival of his city. He went to Sparta and engaged the government in lengthy negotiations, meanwhile instructing all the Athenians in the city, men, women and children, to work unceasingly on the rebuilding of the walls. One can still see today in the walls of the Acropolis drums of broken columns and other debris which were put together so hurriedly and yet very skilfully at that time. The Spartans soon heard rumours of what was going on, but Themistocles assured them that these rumours were greatly exaggerated, until he was able to announce that the fortifications were now completed. The Spartans never forgave him and the Athenians were not long grateful to him. He had powerful enemies in Athens, among whom were Aristides and Pericles' father, Xanthippus, and within a few years he was forced to go into exile. He sought refuge with the King of Persia, who appreciated his great qualities and made him governor of a province.

It had been Themistocles who saw first and most clearly that the political future of Athens was to depend on sea power. He was virtually the creator of the Athenian navy, which had saved Greece in the Persian War; he fortified Piraeus and was said to have declared that, if he could have his way, the Athenians would abandon the time-honoured city around the Acropolis and all move down to the sea. Such a suggestion would certainly offend the more conservatively-minded Athenians and it is likely too that Xanthippus and other members of the leading families would be even more offended by what was, in fact, a necessary and inevitable result of putting more man-power into the fleet. Athenian military power was in future to depend at least as much on the steersmen and sailors in the navy as on the army of cavalry and heavy infantry and it was natural that 'the naval rabble', as the aristocrats called them, would demand an equal share of political power with the richer members of the middle and upper classes. This inevitably led to a widening of the democracy.

Another and almost inevitable result of the policy of Themistocles was that at some time or other there would be a clash with Sparta. A continually growing Athenian power was incompatible with Spartan pretensions to leadership in Greece. Themistocles himself seems to have been perfectly aware of what his policy entailed. As Thucydides, who admired him very greatly, says: 'He was particularly remarkable at looking into the future and seeing there the hidden possibilities for good or evil.'[1]

Pericles, whom Thucydides admires even more than Themistocles, shared this quality, but the aristocrats who opposed Themistocles and who led the state in the years before the emergence of the young Pericles as a leader, while following the expansionist policy of the earlier statesman, seemed curiously unaware of where it was in fact leading them. Particularly remarkable for this kind of political blindness was the brilliant and attractive commander Cimon, the son of Miltiades, the victor of Marathon. Cimon led the forces of the Athenians and their allies to victory after victory over the Persians, constantly increasing the power of Athens and of the men

[1]Thuc. I, 139

Two elders in discussion

in the fleet which he led. At the same time he was fanatically pro-Spartan and generally opposed to political innovation in the direction of a greater degree of democracy.

He was influential enough to be able to lead, in 464, a large Athenian army to the help of Sparta in her most desperate hour of need. The Spartans had suffered enormous casualties in an earthquake and at the same time had to fight for their very existence against a revolt of their subjects. It was a generous action for the Athenians to take and it is exceedingly doubtful whether, if Athens herself had been equally threatened, the Spartans would have shown similar generosity. They certainly failed to show gratitude. After a time, according to Thucydides, they became alarmed by 'the enterprise and unorthodoxy of the Athenians' and feared that their continued presence might have a disturbing and revolutionary effect upon their allies. So, while keeping the rest of their allies with them, they asked the Athenians to go home, merely saying that they needed them no longer.

Naturally the Athenians both in the army and at home felt insulted. The effect of the incident was to discredit Cimon, Sparta's most loyal friend in Athens, and to reverse the general pro-Spartan policy that had been followed up to this time. Before long Cimon was exiled and, though he was recalled later and was again to lead an Athenian fleet against the Persians, he never recovered his political power. The policy of Athens, both at home and abroad, was in future to be guided by Pericles until the time of his death some 30 years later and two and a half years after the outbreak of the Great War between Athens and Sparta.

This policy was to be an amplification of that of Themistocles – expansion abroad and a more and more thorough-going democracy at home. Some aspects of his foreign policy will be considered later. Here I shall merely attempt to discuss what seems to have been Pericles' theory of democracy. Before doing so, however, it is well to note that his foreign and home policy are inextricably bound together. The democracy was an imperialistic democracy; the empire was a democratic imperialism. And though Pericles genuinely believed that Athens gave more than she received from her allies, or subjects (they could be considered either way), she was jealous of her citizenship, preferring to restrict it rather than to extend it, and there was no question at all of allowing those states which originally had joined the alliance voluntarily to break away from their obligations later.

This policy of compulsion was not initiated by Pericles. Quite early in the history of the alliance there had been states which, considering that they had already got all they wanted from the Confederacy, saw no reason to go on sending ships or contributing money to the general fund, and had attempted to secede. Cimon himself had led expeditions against these states and had forced them to return to their allegiance and pay indemnities or increased amounts of annual contributions. The argument justifying this coercion of supposedly independent states was a reasonable one. So long as the war with Persia was still being fought and there were still Greek cities to be liberated, the purposes for which the alliance had originally been formed had not yet been carried out and no secession of a member state could occur without weaken-

The last traces of the Long Walls, which joined Athens to her port, the Piraeus. About four miles long and 200 yards apart, they were built between 461 and 456.

ing the alliance as a whole. It was equally certain, of course, that any secession would also weaken the steadily growing power of Athens herself, and, as time went on, there were more and more complaints that, since the danger from Persia was virtually ended, the money and the man-power of the allies were being exploited solely in the interests of Athens.

The answer given by Pericles to this criticism is a perfectly clear one, though it is not one that will commend itself to doctrinaire liberals of the present day. Certainly it runs counter to much popular thinking about self-determination, since it accepts the fact, which is tacitly understood (though not frequently proclaimed) by all statesmen of major powers, that a great power cannot under any circumstances allow itself to be dangerously weakened in a vital area. Pericles states this fact with greater frankness than is often done today. The last of his great speeches recorded by Thucydides was made to the Athenians after the first and most destructive year of the plague, of which he himself was to die before many months had passed. At this time the Athenians were profoundly discouraged and, because of their sufferings in the plague rather than because of any defeat in war, some were suggesting a policy of peace at any price. In a speech which had the desired effect of stiffening their resolution against the enemy, Pericles has this to say about his own conception of empire:

It is right and proper for you to support the imperial dignity of Athens. This is something in which you all take pride, and you cannot continue to enjoy the privileges unless you also shoulder the burdens of empire. And do not imagine that what we are fighting for is simply the question of freedom or slavery: there is also involved the loss of our empire and the dangers arising from the hatred which we have incurred in administering it. Nor is it any longer possible for you to give up this empire, though there may be some people who in a mood of sudden panic and in a spirit of political apathy actually think that this would be a fine and noble thing to do. In fact you now hold your empire down by force: it may have been wrong to take it; it is certainly dangerous to let it go. And the kind of people who talk of doing so and persuade others to adopt their point of view would very soon bring a state to ruin, and would still do so even if they lived by themselves in isolation. For those who are politically apathetic can only survive if they are supported by people who are capable of taking action. They are quite valueless in a city which controls an empire, though they would be safe slaves in a city that was controlled by others.

A little later in the same speech he goes further still. The fervour and sincerity of his words are quite unmistakeable. They are not words which many statesmen would dare to use today. He continues:

Remember, too, that the reason why Athens has the greatest name in all the world is because she has never given in to adversity, but has spent more life and labour in warfare than any other state, thus winning the greatest power that has ever existed in history, such a power that will be remembered for ever by posterity, even if now (since all things are born to decay) there should come a time when we are forced to yield: yet still it will be remembered that of all Hellenic powers we held the widest sway over the Hellenes, that we stood firm in the greatest wars against their combined forces and against individual

The Treasure House of the Athenians at Delphi. Many city-states erected and filled such a building for the oracle from the spoils of war. The original of this one was created from the plunder at Marathon.

states, that we lived in a city which had been perfectly equipped in every direction and which was the greatest in Hellas.

No doubt all this will be disparaged by people who are politically apathetic; but those who, like us, prefer a life of action will try to imitate us, and, if they fail to secure what we have secured, they will envy us. All who have taken upon themselves to rule over others have incurred hatred and unpopularity for a time; but if one has a great aim to pursue, this burden of envy must be accepted, and it is wise to accept it. Hatred does not last for long; but the brilliance of the present is the glory of the future stored up for ever in the memory of man. It is for you to safeguard that future glory and to do nothing now that is dishonourable.[1]

[1]Thuc. II, 63–4

The passing of a warrior. LEFT: *Athenian, c.440. Death and Sleep, winged youths, stoop to lift a young hero whose gravestone has his helmet drawn upon it. The mood is tender and solemn.* RIGHT: *Spartan, c.525. Slung over the shoulders of two cheerful survivors the corpse is lugged from the battlefield in a procession.*

Pericles' statement is clear enough, but it is possible, indeed easy, entirely to mis-understand him unless we can free our minds from some modern and conventional ways of political thinking. Because Pericles takes pride in the military achievement of Athens and in the extent and efficiency of her empire, because he admits that in building and holding this empire she has incurred hatred, but nevertheless declares that, whatever the rights and wrongs of that may be, it would be both dangerous and dishonourable to allow the empire to slip from her grasp, it is easy to imagine many people who would hurl at him the abusive epithets of 'war-monger' and 'imperialist' and would so dismiss him from their minds.

They would be wrong to do so, even though it is true that arguments which do bear a superficial resemblance to those of Pericles can and have been used to justify naked aggression or to glorify bad causes. Thucydides, himself, as we shall see, gives us plenty of examples of this, and notably in the speeches and character of Cleon and in the arguments of the Athenian ambassadors at Melos. Thucydides hates and despises Cleon almost as much as he honours and admires Pericles, yet we find Cleon in some of his most cynical and brutal speeches using arguments which, looked at superficially, may seem quite like those of Pericles. In fact, as Thucydides means us to see and as he often states himself, the difference is enormous.

One may note, to begin with, in nearly all of Pericles' political pronouncements something that has already been noticed in Aeschylus – a combination of a very ancient tradition with a startling modernity. The aristocratic concepts of honour and dishonour, glory and disgrace, are much more frequently used than any words which could be translated as 'good' and 'evil'. At the same time the applications of these concepts are not confined to the individual hero, as in Homer, but concern a consciously modern democracy in which each man has both his rights and his duties.

The imperial power of Athens has, in Pericles' view, 'a great aim to pursue'. Precisely what this great aim is, we shall consider later. Here it is enough to say that the aim is neither selfish nor cynical nor vindictive, as it was to become at a later stage of the war. It is concerned with 'the glory of the future' and with 'a city perfectly equipped in every direction'.

The justification for Athenian power over others is to be found mainly in the greatness of the aim, but also in the proved ability of the Athenians to pursue it successfully. It is accepted as axiomatic that in human societies some people do, in fact, rule over others. Athens is distinguished from other leaders, past or present, by the fact that she uses her power efficiently in the direction of her 'great aim' and moderately in regard to those whom she controls. As Pericles says in his funeral speech, which will be examined later, 'We make friends by doing good to others, not by receiving good from them',[1] and he emphasises the aristocratic spirit in which this is carried out: 'We are unique in this. When we do kindnesses to others, we do not do them out of any calculations of profit or loss: we do them without afterthought, relying on our free liberality.'

As we shall see, this spirit of free liberality is something very seldom found among

[1] Thuc, II, 40

the Athenian statesmen who came after Pericles. In taking from Pericles one part of his political theory and entirely rejecting the other, they of course distorted the whole into a sad parody of what was certainly in the eyes of Thucydides a noble and a practicable ideal.

What Cleon and the rest did take from Pericles was his insistence that, whatever the rights and wrongs of holding imperial power, it was certainly dangerous to relinquish it, although, in fact, their own greed, ambition and stupidity led them to act in just the ways which Pericles had warned them against and finally to a disaster which would have been impossible, had Pericles' advice been followed.

Pericles' insistence on the necessity of holding the empire is expressed, to a modern mind somewhat brutally, in the phrase: 'it may have been wrong to take it; it is certainly dangerous to let it go'. He admits that 'You now hold your empire down by force', and that hatred has been incurred in administering it. Personally I find this frankness very refreshing, but, as already stated, it is very important to realise that these words, coming from Pericles, mean something completely different from what they would mean if spoken by Cleon.

It is fair to say, I think, that when Pericles states that it may have been wrong to take the empire, he means simply that, in the present context, the question of rights and wrongs in the original formation of the empire are no longer of any practical importance. We can be certain, in fact, that in accepting the leadership of the allied forces operating against Persia, Pericles considered that Athens was acting rightly as well as wisely; and most historians would agree with him. But, as Pericles says, whether this first step in the direction of empire was or was not legitimate is, at the time of the outbreak of the war with Sparta, beside the point. The empire is by this time a fact and a fact on which not only the greatness but the survival of Athens depends. Athens cannot exist without food and material imported from abroad; her supplies of these necessities depend on her sea power, which itself depends on a chain of friendly bases along the trade routes, particularly those in the eastern and northern Aegean and the Hellespont. These are absolutely vital interests and must on no account be jeopardised. Those who think that 'it would be a fine and noble thing' to give up the power, the bases and the authority which safeguard these vital interests are, in Pericles' view, blind to the facts and, if they had their own way, would soon bring ruin on the whole state, including themselves.

Assuming that the facts are as Pericles represents them, his argument is, to say the least, respectable. It is certain that Thucydides thought it to be not only respectable, but accurate and inspiring. The accuracy is in the truthful estimate of the political, military and economic conditions and trends of the time. The inspiration is to be found in that other part of Pericles' political theory, 'the greatness of the aim', on which so far we have scarcely touched. And the tragedy implicit in Thucydides' history is in the rapidly increasing separation of the two parts of Pericles' political theory after his death, so that in the end the greatness of the aim was forgotten or vulgarised and was replaced by the mere brutalities and self-seeking of the politics of greed and power.

Many modern and ancient theorists would say that this process is inevitable, that the exercise of power, even when reasoned and generous, as Pericles claims his own to be, must always corrupt. Thucydides himself, though he certainly believed that Pericles was uncorrupted by power, would agree that, as he says, 'human nature being what it is', the possibility of the corruption and degradation of any standard or ideal is always present. Pericles too, as we have seen, admits that 'since all things are born to decay' there is a possibility, remote as it seems to him, that Athens may be defeated in the war. Even so, he reflects, the great experiment will have been worth the making; the efforts and the sacrifices will have been justified by visible, tangible and lasting achievement; 'the brilliance of the present is the glory of the future stored up for ever in the memory of man'. The words and the sentiment are in the aristocratic and Homeric tradition; they are spoken in the context of the modern politics of his times.

Nearly all our knowledge of Pericles comes, of course, from Thucydides. Pericles himself left no written work behind him, and, apart from the speeches of his which have been reported by Thucydides, only a very few quotations in other authors survive. There is, for instance, a phrase from a speech made in honour of the Athenians who had fallen in the war with Samos, which took place some years before the outbreak of the war with Sparta. On this occasion Pericles is reported to have said, 'It seems to us that the spring has gone out of the year'. Such poetical phrases, occurring in the course of a careful and logical analysis, are frequent in the speeches of Pericles reported by Thucydides. They are unlike Thucydides' own style or the style of other speakers in his history. It seems very likely, then, that the words which Thucydides puts into Pericles' mouth were, in fact, the very words which he used. We know the importance which Thucydides attached to accurate reporting; it is likely that he listened himself to every speech of Pericles which he reports and certain that very many of his readers would have done so.

In a passage which must have been written almost thirty years after the speeches of Pericles which he records, Thucydides, in the light of after events, gives us his final judgment on the great statesman whom he had admired in his youth and whom he still admires. He writes as follows:[1]

> Indeed, during the whole period of peace time when Pericles was at the head of affairs the state was wisely led and firmly guarded, and it was under him that Athens was at her greatest. And when the war broke out, here, too, he appears to have accurately estimated what the power of Athens was. He survived the outbreak of war by two years and six months, and after his death his foresight with regard to the war became even more evident. For Pericles had said that Athens would be victorious if she bided her time and took care of her navy, if she avoided trying to add to the empire during the course of the war, and if she did nothing to risk the safety of the city itself. But his successors did the exact opposite, and in other matters which apparently had no connexion with the war private ambition and private profit led to policies which were bad both for the Athenians themselves and for their allies. Such policies, when successful,

[1]Thuc. II, 65

only brought credit and advantage to individuals, and when they failed, the whole war potential of the state was impaired. The reason for this was that Pericles, because of his position, his intelligence, and his known integrity, could respect the liberty of the people and at the same time hold them in check. It was he who led them, rather than they who led him, and, since he never sought power from any wrong motive, he was under no necessity of flattering them: in fact he was so highly respected that he was able to speak angrily to them and to contradict them. Certainly when he saw that they were going too far in a mood of over-confidence, he would bring back to them a sense of their dangers: and when they were discouraged for no good reason he would restore their confidence. So, in what was nominally a democracy, power was really in the hands of the first citizen. But his successors, who were more on a level with each other and each of whom aimed at occupying the first place, adopted methods of demagogy which resulted in their losing control over the actual conduct of affairs.

If Pericles, from another world, had been able to read these words, he would have been forced to agree that Thucydides' account of those who came after him was perfectly accurate. But it is very unlikely that he would have approved of the phrase 'in what was nominally a democracy'. To him, as we shall see and as Thucydides has already told us, the democracy was anything but nominal. It was real, as no other political system could be. In fact it was more than a political system; it was a way of life and the best way of life ever discovered by man.

But he would have been far more shocked by the remarks about democracy made by his young and brilliant kinsman, Alcibiades, who, on one important occasion, speaks of democracy as 'a system which is generally recognised as absurd'.[1]

Before many years had passed the 'absurdity' of the system would be recognised by Plato, a more profound thinker, though a less able politician, than Alcibiades. And many thinkers, both ancient and modern, would agree with him. Many too, while defending democracy, defend it on the grounds that it is the least of a number of evils. It is admitted that democracy is bound to be, in many ways, inefficient and cumbrous. Ideally a government in the hands of a committee of honest experts would do more good more quickly than a government in which everyone has a voice. But, it is contended, though such a committee, or even a dictator, may be and has often been shown to be excellent for a time, experience proves that in the end such governments will degenerate into tyranny and the people will lose their freedom, which is, or should be, their most cherished possession. Democracy does guarantee freedom and is therefore the least bad of all systems of government so far designed by man.

Alcibiades, Plato and even Thucydides would dispute the statement that democracy is a necessary guarantor of freedom. They had all seen the Athenian democracy act with a stupidity and intolerance as great as any tyrant. But they might agree that, with certain safeguards, the rest of the argument does have some force. Pericles, on the other hand, would utterly reject it. To him the Athenian democracy was not the least of evils, but the greatest of goods.

[1] Thuc. VI, 89

THE GREAT AIM

The funeral speech of Pericles,[1] which is recorded by Thucydides, was made at the end of the first year of the war. In praising the dead and the city for which they died, Pericles constantly recurs to the unique quality of the Athenian way of life and the complete contrast which it presents to that of the Spartans. The speech is much more than propaganda to suit an immediate purpose. It is a clear statement of the great aim which, in Pericles' view, justifies Athenian power and ennobles the sacrifices which have been and are being made to retain it. Most of the speeches reported by Thucydides are set down with little or no introduction, but in this case he evidently wishes to emphasise the importance of the occasion and goes out of his way to describe the scene and to place it in the context of a long and proud tradition. He writes:

In the same winter the Athenians, following their ancient custom, gave a public funeral for those who had been the first to die in the war. These funerals are held in the following way: two days before the ceremony the bones of the fallen are brought and put in a tent which has been erected, and people make whatever offerings they wish to their own dead. Then there is a funeral procession in which coffins of cypress wood are carried on waggons. There is one coffin for each tribe, which contains the bones of members of that tribe. One empty bier is decorated and carried in the procession: this is for the missing, whose bodies could not be recovered. Everyone who wishes to, both citizens and foreigners, can join in the procession, and the women who are related to the dead are there to make their laments at the tomb. The bones are laid in the public burying-place, which is in the most beautiful quarter outside the city walls. Here the Athenians always bury those who have fallen in war. The only exception is those who died at Marathon, who, because their achievement was considered absolutely outstanding, were buried on the battlefield itself.

When the bones have been laid in the earth, a man chosen by the city for his intellectual gifts and for his general reputation makes an appropriate speech in praise of the dead, and after the speech all depart. This is the procedure at these burials, and all through the war, when the time came to do so, the Athenians followed this ancient custom. Now, at

[1]Thuc. II, 34–6

Gravestones were often as beautiful as they were durable. This represents the deceased husband and wife.

Part of a funeral procession depicted on a tomb

the burial of those who were the first to fall in the war Pericles, the son of Xanthippus, was chosen to make the speech. When the moment arrived, he came forward from the tomb and, standing on a high platform, so that he might be heard by as many people as possible in the crowd, he spoke as follows:

He begins by confessing the difficulty or impossibility of doing justice to his theme. However the tradition must be followed and he will do his best.

I shall begin by speaking about our ancestors, since it is only right and proper on such an occasion to pay them the honour of recalling what they did. In this land of ours there have always been the same people living from generation to generation up till now, and they, by their courage and their virtues, have handed it on to us a free country. They certainly deserve our praise. Even more so do our fathers deserve it. For to the inheritance they had received they added all the empire we have now, and it was not without blood and toil that they handed it down to us of the present generation. And then we ourselves, assembled here today, who are mostly in the prime of life, have, in most directions, added to the power of our empire and have organised our state in such a way that it is perfectly well able to look after itself both in peace and in war.

Here again we may notice that Pericles starts by emphasising the antiquity of the Athenian tradition, but he goes on to imply that the really great achievements have been modern, indeed the work of the last two or three generations.

He continues by saying that he does not propose to go into any detail about the history of how this happened, since the story is familiar to his hearers. Instead, he says, 'What I want to do is, in the first place, to discuss the spirit in which we faced our trials and also our constitution and the way of life which has made us great. After that I shall speak in praise of the dead, believing that this kind of speech is not inappropriate to the present occasion, and that this whole assembly, of citizens and foreigners, may listen to it with advantage.'

And as he begins to speak about the constitution and way of life of the Athenians, he emphasises from the start the fact that Athens, from her long tradition, has evolved a constitution which is something entirely new:

> Let me say that our system of government does not copy the institutions of our neigh-bours. It is more the case of our being a model to others than of our imitating anyone else. Our constitution is called a democracy because power is in the hands not of a minority but of the whole people. When it is a question of settling private disputes, everyone is equal before the law; when it is a question of putting one person before another in positions of public responsibility, what counts is not membership of a parti-cular class, but the actual ability which the man possesses. No one, so long as he has it in him to be of service to the state, is kept in political obscurity because of poverty.

'To be of service to the state' was, as all Pericles' hearers would know, the acknow-ledged aim of the Spartan discipline. So also was a rigid obedience to the laws. But, in Pericles' view, there was something mechanical and inhuman in the Spartan ideal. In the following passage he emphasises the ease, tolerance and flexibility of the Athenian way of life:

> And just as our political life is free and open, so is our day-to-day life in our relations with each other. We do not get into a state with our next-door neighbour if he enjoys himself in his own way, nor do we give him the kind of black looks which, though they do no real harm, still do hurt people's feelings. We are free and tolerant in our private lives: but in public affairs we keep to the law. This is because it commands our deep respect.
>
> We give our obedience to those whom we put in positions of authority, and we obey the laws themselves, especially those which are for the protection of the oppressed, and those unwritten laws which it is an acknowledged shame to break.

It has often been noticed that in all the literature of fifth-century Athens, full as it is of patriotic feeling, there are hardly any references to the great architecture, for most of which Pericles was personally responsible, or to the festivals of poetry and

drama – things which in subsequent ages down to our own day have been by visitors, tourists and scholars recognised as wonders of the world. Pericles does indeed allude to them, but not in the reverent tones of the archaeologist or the art critic. To him they are a natural part of the Athenian way of life and something to be enjoyed, like the amenities of household furniture or the imports which depend on good harbours and a vigorous mercantile marine. He says:

> And here is another point. When our work is over, we are in a position to enjoy all kinds of recreation for our spirits. There are various kinds of contests and sacrifices regularly throughout the year; in our own homes we find a beauty and a good taste which delight us every day and which drive away our cares. Then the greatness of our city brings it about that all the good things from all over the world flow in to us, so that to us it seems just as natural to enjoy foreign goods as our own local products.

He now begins a more specific account of the differences between Sparta and Athens. The Spartans, a comparatively small and highly disciplined military caste, holding down a large subject population, were mistrustful of strangers. They would deport or secretly put to death aliens who might at any time seem to them likely to become dangerous. Athens is, on the other hand, according to Pericles an open city and the liberal education of her citizens has more advantages than, and none of the disadvantages of, the Spartan system. His words are:

> Then there is a great difference between us and our opponents, in our attitude to military security. Here are some examples. Our city is open to the world, and we have no periodical deportations in order to prevent people observing or finding out secrets which might be of military advantage to the enemy. This is because we rely, not on secret weapons, but on our own real courage and loyalty. There is a difference, too, in our educational systems. The Spartans, from their earliest boyhood, are submitted to the most laborious training in courage; we pass our lives without all these restrictions, and yet are just as ready to face the same dangers as they are. . . . There are certain advantages, I think, in our way of meeting danger voluntarily, with an easy mind, instead of with a laborious training, with natural rather than with state-induced courage.

In the next paragraph also, Pericles seems to be implying the contrast between the Athenian and Spartan ideal. The Spartans prided themselves on their toughness and on the brevity and pointedness of their laconic utterings. To them the Athenians would seem a nation of talkative intellectuals, spending much too much time on cultural pursuits and on unnecessary political discussions. It was far better, in the Spartan view, to do one's duty and mind one's own business. Pericles replies vigorously to such criticism:

> Our love of what is beautiful does not lead to extravagance; our love for the things of the mind does not make us soft. We regard wealth as something to be properly used rather than as something to boast about. As for poverty, no one need be ashamed to admit it: the real shame is in not taking practical measures to escape from it. Here each

A woman offers a basketful of fruit.

individual is interested not only in his own affairs but in the affairs of the state as well: even those who are mostly occupied with their own business are extremely well-informed on general politics: this is a peculiarity of ours: we do not say that a man who takes no interest in politics is a man who minds his own business; we say that he has no business here at all. We Athenians, in our own persons, take our decisions on policy or submit them to proper discussion, for we do not think that there is any incompatibility between words and deeds: the worst thing is to rush into action before the consequences have been properly debated. And this is another point where we differ from other people. We are capable at the same time of taking risks and of estimating them beforehand. Others are brave out of ignorance and, when they stop to think, they begin to fear. But the man who most truly can be accounted brave is he who best knows the meaning of what is sweet in life and of what is terrible, and then goes out undeterred to meet what is to come.

The last point which Pericles makes in the section of his speech which is devoted to his praise of Athens is one to which we have referred already – his claim that Athens makes friends by doing good to others rather than by receiving good from them and that this is the result, not of calculation, but of her free liberality. He then sums up this part of his argument:

Slaves carrying table and pot. Rather than one large one, many small tables were used and set down where convenient, even for a shared meal.

OPPOSITE: *Sandal-maker cutting the sole round his customer's foot. The trade was limited by many Greeks going barefoot indoors or during the summer.*

Taking everything together then, I declare that our city is an education to Greece, and I declare that in my opinion each single one of our citizens, in all the manifold aspects of life, is able to show himself the rightful lord and owner of his own person, and to do this, moreover, with exceptional grace and exceptional versatility.

This, he goes on to say, is no empty boasting. The evidence is there for all to see. And he concludes this section of his speech with these words:

Mighty indeed are the marks and monuments of our empire which we have left. Future ages will wonder at us, as the present age wonders at us now. We do not need the praises of a Homer, or of anyone else whose words may delight us for a moment, but whose estimation of facts will fall short of what is really true. For our adventurous spirit has forced an entry into every sea and into every land; and everywhere we have left behind us everlasting memorials of good done to our friends or suffering inflicted on our enemies.

Pericles now turns to his praise of those who have died in battle. Here, as elsewhere, we notice the interweaving of the two strands in his thought. One strand seems to come straight from the epic. To die bravely in the face of the enemy is glorious and the final consummation of individual manliness. The heroes in Homer also knew the sweetness of life, but their fear of the reproaches of others was greater than the fear of death, and honour was the sweetest thing of all. So it was with these Athenians. As Pericles says:

As for success or failure, they left that in the doubtful hands of Hope, and when the reality of battle was before their faces, they put their trust in their own selves. In the fighting, they thought it more honourable to stand their ground and suffer death than to give in and save their lives. So they fled from the reproaches of men, abiding with life and limb the brunt of battle; and, in a small moment of time, the climax of their lives, a culmination of glory, not of fear, were swept away from us.

But this personal glory, real as it is, differs in an important respect from the glory sought and won by Achilles or by Hector. These Athenian dead are more than heroes and the reason is that they were, as Pericles says, 'worthy of their city'. It would be easy, he points out, to show how necessary it is to defend oneself against the enemy's attack; but the conduct of these men goes beyond this. They were not merely defenders; they were lovers of Athens.

What I would prefer is that you should fix your eyes every day on the greatness of Athens as she really is, and should fall in love with her. When you realise her greatness, then reflect that what made her great was men with a spirit of adventure, men who knew their duty, men who were ashamed to fall below a certain standard. If they ever failed in an enterprise, they made up their minds that at any rate the city should not find their courage lacking to her, and they gave to her the best contribution that they could. They gave their lives, to her and to all of us, and for their own selves they won praises that never grow old, the most splendid of sepulchres – not the sepulchre in which their bodies are laid, but where their glory remains eternal in men's minds, always there on

Apollo, seen here as the enforcer of order and civilisation on the wild and barbarous

the right occasion to stir others to speech or action. For famous men have the whole earth as their memorial: it is not only the inscriptions on their graves in their own country that mark them out; no, in foreign lands also, not in any visible form but in people's hearts, their memory abides and grows. Make up your minds that happiness depends on being free, and freedom depends on being courageous.

Pericles' final words are spoken in comfort to those who have been bereaved. The parents of those who are dead must be 'well aware that they have grown up in a world where there are many changes and chances. But this is good fortune – for men to end their lives with honour, as these have done, and for you honourably to lament them; their life was set to a measure where death and happiness went hand in hand.'

Again the sentiment is Homeric, but in the poetic quality of the last phrase there is something different and something newer. 'Happiness', to which Pericles often recurs, is not a theme for epic. The phrase may remind us, as it may have reminded some in Pericles' audience, of the contemporary reliefs on gravestones in which the sadness and the inevitability of death are clearly shown, but are somehow suffused with a calm and a resignation, an enduring dignity and sweetness which can indeed suggest a life 'set to a measure where death and happiness went hand in hand'.

Some of those who are now sad, as they must be, because of the death of their children may still, Pericles goes on, find some comfort in having other children who will cheer their homes and alleviate their sorrow. And this 'will be a help to the city, too, both in filling the empty places and in assuring her security. For it is impossible for a man to put forward fair and honest views about our affairs if he has not, like everyone else, children whose lives may be at stake.'

But there will be others who are too old to have any more children. To them Pericles has this to say:

> I would ask you to count as gain the greater part of your life, in which you have been happy, and remember that what remains is not long, and let your hearts be lifted up at the thought of the fair fame of the dead. One's sense of honour is the only thing that does not grow old, and the last pleasure, when one is worn out with age, is not, as the poet said, making money, but having the respect of one's fellow men.

After a few words to the sons, brothers and widows of the dead, Pericles concludes his speech:

> I have now, as the law demanded, said what I had to say. For the time being our offerings to the dead have been made, and for the future their children will be supported at the public expense by the city, until they come of age. This is the crown and prize which she offers, both to the dead and to their children, for the ordeals which they have faced. Where the rewards of valour are the greatest, there you will find also the best and bravest spirits among the people. And now, when you have mourned your dear ones, you must depart.

In this speech of Pericles, which may be considered as his political testament,

The Greek profile, perhaps of Aphrodite. The hole near the ear is to attach the disc as a wall-ornament.

LEFT: *Boy with hare. Hares were common as pets and a favoured present between lovers.* CENTRE: *The perils of drink. A sympathetic girl, lightly-dressed, holds the head of a vomiting boy, who is clad in a heavier cloak.* RIGHT: *The flautist half joins the dancing of his companion, who has a pair of castanets.*

many passages may be found which might be quoted with approval, and indeed have often been imitated, by statesmen in later times who have believed in a mystique of 'the State' as a kind of divinity from which the individual draws his life and to which he should be wholly subservient; and there are also many passages which have long been the stock-in-trade of liberal individualists – 'equality before the law', 'equality of opportunity', 'the rights of the individual', and even, though Pericles would not have put it that way, 'academic freedom'. But it is perfectly clear that Pericles is not, in a modern sense, either an 'individualist' or a political absolutist. Each of these terms implies a conflict between the individual and the state. To Pericles this conflict simply did not exist in Athens, although it certainly did in the opposing state of Sparta, where the individual was, from an early age, constricted and limited by a discipline which had no other aim except the perpetuation of the military and ethical tradition into which he had been born. It was a system which, later on, was to appeal to Plato and to Xenophon. To Pericles it was the antithesis of what he found great and noble in Athens. The individual qualities which the Spartans so distrusted and feared were just the qualities which Pericles respected and admired, namely the

ability to show oneself 'in all the manifold aspects of life . . . the rightful lord and owner of his own person, and to do this, moreover, with exceptional grace and exceptional versatility'.

But Pericles is not only contemptuous of the Spartan ideal. He is equally contemptuous of any ideal which neglects, denies or weakens the vitality of the city. Anyone who prides himself on 'minding his own business' has, he says, 'no business here at all'. An Athenian can love beauty without falling into the luxury of extravagance and he can love the things of the mind and be in no danger of becoming soft; but these immunities depend on his free devotion to the city, whose affairs he handles himself in co-operation with others and with which, seeing her greatness 'as it really is', he has fallen in love. Like any lover, he will be prepared to sacrifice his life for her, if that is required of him. No one has ever praised those who have died for their country more eloquently than Pericles, and yet it should be remembered that what he chiefly valued was the living. He prided himself as a general on causing no casualties that could possibly be avoided; and on his deathbed, according to Plutarch,[1] when his

[1]*Lives,* 'Pericles', XXXVIII, 4

friends were talking of the victories he had won and of the trophies which he had set up, he remarked that many generals had won victories and in these there was always an element of luck. What he was really proud of, he said, was that 'no living Athenian has ever had to put on mourning because of me'.

Pericles was at least as aware as Sophocles, or anyone else, that 'it is not ships or walls, but men who make the city'. But, in common with nearly all Greeks of his time, he considered that a man without a city was a poor and stunted thing. Man makes the city, but the city, and especially Athens, also makes the man. Even such great political theorists as Plato and Aristotle were unable to imagine any organisation other than the city-state which could as well or better secure for human beings a happy, full and good life. And this predilection of theirs was not the result of ignorance or blindness. They knew the history of Egypt and they had long been familiar with the huge, centralized and often very efficiently organized empire of Persia. The

The husband returns late and drunk but his wife is far from indignant, indeed she seems so nervous as to be wondering whether she dare let him in.

new Greek empire of Macedonia was almost within their sight. Yet, although they acknowledged and respected some elements in the structure of these great powers, they still regarded them as wholly inferior, for the purpose of living – which was the aim of politics – to the comparatively small and independent Greek cities in which they had been brought up.

For this attitude of theirs they have been severely censured by modern writers. 'If only', it is often said, 'the Greeks had been able to unite, instead of ruining everything by constant wars among themselves; if only their great leaders and theorists had recognised the necessity of sacrificing some degree of autonomy among the individual states to the general interest and advanced in the direction of thinking in terms of federalism or nationalism, then their great promise would not have ended in failure and they might not have been submerged by the great powers first of Macedonia and later of Rome.'

A dancing lesson

The same argument is often used with regard to the national states of today and there is, no doubt, some force in it. It is perfectly true that the Athens which Pericles loved never fully recovered from the effects of the war with Sparta. But whether this Athens or the Greek experiment in general 'ended in failure' is quite another question. The empire of Alexander was something different from the Athenian empire or alliance; but it was still Greek and was still, to a large extent, organised on the ideals of the city. Nor was Greece, in any except a political sense, submerged by Rome. She civilised the Romans and, as Pericles might say, gave far more than she received. These points certainly deserve consideration. A large and unified political structure undoubtedly possesses solid advantages over small and fiercely autonomous

A game of hockey. Ball games were played, but overshadowed by athletics.

organisations which are incapable of acting together. Yet, as we saw in the story of Zeus and Prometheus, Power, however efficiently organised, is not the same thing as Justice, and Authority without Freedom is as dangerous as Freedom without Authority. An imposed uniformity may have much to offer in the way of peace, quiet and security, but it scarcely meets the requirements of those who, in Pericles' words, 'prefer a life of action'.

This life of action is, as we have seen, natural to Pericles and those like him. Its great aim is both the greatness and splendour of the city and the happiness, courage, wisdom and versatility of each citizen. These qualities in the citizen go together with the greatness of the city and are so 'set to a measure' that neither can exist without

the other. And, as Pericles constantly insists, this great aim has already been achieved. Athens, at the time of the outbreak of the war, is already 'an education to Greece'. She does not need the praises even of a Homer or of any one else, 'whose estimation of facts will fall short of what is really true'.

Pericles accepts as axiomatic that glory, when deserved, is worth having and that great things cannot be done without effort and without sacrifice. The deserved glory and the greatness of the things done justify the effort and ennoble the sacrifice.

As to the question of whether the glory that Athens enjoys is really deserved, Pericles is content to let the facts speak for themselves. The facts are both in the achievements and in the character of the Athenian people. That Athens rules over others is obvious and, in his view, necessary not only for the fulfilment of her great aim, but for her survival. But, he says, 'in her case, and in her case alone . . . no subject can complain of being governed by people unfit for their responsibilities'.

As for the charge that he has unnecessarily involved his people in war, Pericles' answers, given on several occasions, are consistent. In his last recorded speech he says: 'If one has a free choice and can live undisturbed, it is sheer folly to go to war. But suppose the choice was forced upon one – submission and immediate slavery or danger with the hope of survival – then I prefer the man who stands up to danger rather than the one who runs away from it.'[1]

It is, of course, still possible to contend that Pericles' estimate of the achievement and value of Athens is incorrect, or that he has misjudged the nature of the choice between peace and war which was set before her. Thucydides, who was in a good position to judge, did not think so. And most modern historians would agree with him, although it is perfectly true that in the later years of the war after Pericles' death Athens on at least one occasion rejected an honourable peace when it was offered to her and in matters of imperial policy failed to live up to the standard which Pericles had set before her.

It would be possible, too, to say that no war can ever be justified or that all power exercised over others is wrong. But unless one were to adopt such extreme attitudes of pacifism or quietism, it is hard to see how the modern abusive epithets 'imperialist' and 'war-monger' can properly be applied to Pericles.

A more searching criticism and one which, as we shall see, can be supported by evidence from Thucydides himself may be made from a consideration of the real limitations of human nature. Did Pericles expect the impossible? Granted that cities and individuals can rise to great heights of sacrifice, virtue and intelligence, can they remain on these heights for long? Can any system of government or education ensure the continuance of that precise balance or measure in which patriotism and initiative go happily together? Can a whole people exercise power with the precision of an expert and with the aristocratic generosity that is not always found even amongst an élite? Unless, whatever the name given to the political organisation, they are in fact firmly led in a chosen direction by one man or by a few with outstanding gifts and perfect integrity, will they not inevitably act foolishly as the result of divided counsels,

[1]Thuc. II, 61

or viciously as the result of the greed, self-indulgence, laziness and arrogance which are at least as common amongst men as the higher virtues and are particularly common when there is any relaxation of control?

These questions were frequently debated in Pericles' own day and were even more fully debated in the years after his death and in the following century. Most of the answers given were pessimistic. Those who gave the answers had seen, as Thucydides had seen, the decline and the degeneration in everything except courage of the Athens described in Pericles' funeral speech. Thucydides, unlike Plato, still retained his ardent admiration for Pericles himself, and is convinced that, had Pericles been still able to control affairs, the disasters which he records could never have taken place; but this claim is in itself an admission of the instability of the system which Pericles had praised.

Pericles' own answer to such criticisms as those which we have outlined has, in part, been given already and the rest is easy to surmise. To the assertion that the system of life which he praises is an impossibility, he would reply that, so far from being an impossibility, it was a fact. But he would not claim that the system is self-perpetuating and eternal. The faults in human nature are real and nothing good can last without vigilance, effort and activity. He admits that, 'since all things are born to decay', this system of Athenian life will not last for ever, although he sees no immediate danger of its breaking down. What is important is that it has existed and does exist and will enjoy the only immortality possible to man and his creations; 'the brilliance of the present is the glory of the future, stored up for ever in the memory of man.'

BUILDING OF THE PARTHENON

Pericles, as has been noted, makes in his funeral speech only a passing reference to the great buildings of Athens, for which he was chiefly responsible himself and which have amazed and delighted generations who have come after him. Thucydides is equally reticent. In fact his only reference to these glories of architecture is by way of an illustration of his contention that 'we have no right . . . to judge cities by their appearance rather than by their actual power'. Supposing, he says, that nothing remained of Athens and Sparta except for their buildings, one might conclude that Sparta was a poor place, whereas in fact she was extremely powerful, and that Athens 'from what met the eye had been twice as powerful as in fact it was'.[1]

One can imagine how differently Cicero would have behaved, if he had stood in Pericles' place; and imagination reels at the thought of the speeches he would have made if he personally, like Pericles, could have claimed the credit for so much of what met the eye.

But the reticence of Pericles and Thucydides does not mean that either they or their fellow citizens were in the least indifferent to the architecture, sculpture, painting and poetry which were constantly before them and which played so large a part in their lives. They were not, like Cicero, forced to look back to a culture which was in the past; the culture was alive, present and growing all round them. It was not stored away in museums and libraries, but was seen and keenly discussed by everyone. Like everything else, it was part of politics, the life of the city.

The great building programme, and in particular the building of the Parthenon, was not only a part of politics in general, but was a point at issue between Pericles and the conservative opposition. This opposition was led by Thucydides, the son of Melesias, a relation of Cimon and, in all probability, also of Thucydides the historian, who, as we have seen, unlike the rest of his family, seems to have had nothing but admiration both for Pericles and for his policy. The opposition led by Thucydides, the son of Melesias, was aristocratic in the sense that it was pro-Spartan, as Cimon had been. But it accepted, as Cimon had not accepted, the fact that a rapidly expand-

[1]Thuc. I, 10

Pentelic marble from which the Parthenon, inter alia, *was built*

A Model of the Acropolis in the Fifth Century

1 *Parthenon of Pericles, 447–438* 2 *West Court of Parthenon* 3 *Chalkotheke, storage place for arms, completed c.450* 4 *Artemis Brauronia, c.460* 5 *Temple of Athena Nike, 450–425?* 6 *Propylaea, c.437–432* 7 *Bronze Athena, 465–c.455* 8 *Arrhephoreion* 9 *Pandroseion* 10 *Erechtheum, 421–406* 11 *Altar of Athena, c.520, restored after 479, destroyed 400?* 12 *Klepsydra Fountain*

ing Athenian power was incompatible with a policy of peace and friendship with Sparta. Cimon had done almost as much as Pericles did later to extend and consolidate the empire. Most of his great victories had been won against the Persians and served to liberate Greeks under Persian subjugation. He seems to have been curiously blind to the fact that these patriotic achievements, which also and inevitably resulted in an alteration of the balance of power between Sparta and Athens, would certainly arouse among the Spartans not generous applause, but fear, jealousy and misgiving.

In 448, shortly after Cimon's death, peace was concluded with Persia and the original purpose of the Athenian alliance had been carried out: the Greeks of Asia Minor had been liberated. Six years before this time the allied treasury had been transferred, on the pretext, not unreasonable at that date, of greater security, from Delos to Athens and the funds were now entirely under Athenian management. Part of these funds was applied by Pericles to a programme which included rebuilding the temples destroyed by the Persians, strengthening the fortifications linking Athens with Piraeus and other projects.

Plutarch[1] seems to have been shocked by the way the opposition attacked Pericles for what they considered as an unnecessary and illegal waste of other people's money on these projects. He implies that the attacks were malicious and slanderous and emphasises the fact that these great buildings were and are beautiful and delightful and constitute now the chief evidence to prove that the power and splendour of Athens really were what they have been said to be. But Plutarch, living under the early Roman empire, is writing rather as an antiquarian and a sightseer than as one engaged in the politics of the time. And for us it is impossible to say to what extent the tactics of the opposition depended on a sincere interest in the allies and a demand for financial probity and how far they were a political manoeuvre designed to further a pro-Spartan policy and to weaken the growing power of Pericles in the assembly in Athens. The opposition argument was, according to Plutarch, that the democracy had disgraced itself and was getting a bad name because of the removal of the common fund from Delos to Athens. It was an insult to Greece and a clear sign that she was being subjected to a kind of tyranny when people could see that contributions which had been enforced in order to carry on the war with Persia were now being used by Athens 'to gild herself and to deck herself out, like a common prostitute, loading herself with expensive jewellery and statues and temples costing millions'.

In reply to this, Plutarch goes on, Pericles would instruct the people that they had absolutely no obligation to account for the way they spent the money which they received. So long as Athens, to whom fell far the greatest share of the fighting, fulfilled her promise to keep Greece free from the Persians, no one could complain. Once she had done this, it was only right that she should use the surplus on works which, when finished, would bring her everlasting glory and, while they were being made, would stimulate every art and give everyone useful employment.

This is not an argument that would satisfy a modern accountant, but it satisfied the Athenians. In 443 Pericles' opponent Thucydides was ostracised and went into

[1] *Lives*, 'Pericles', XII

exile. For the rest of his life, with one short interval, Pericles was in complete control. In his building programme his aim was, as Plutarch says, both practical, to give employment to those not serving in the army, navy or administration, and also, as was his whole policy, in the direction of 'everlasting glory'. Plutarch also credits him with the moral intention of putting an end to any idleness and laziness that there might be in the city, but here he is probably thinking of his own day and of the undoubtedly lazy demanders of bread and circuses in Rome. In the fifth century nobody ever accused the Athenians of being lazy. The complaint was rather that they were far too active. Certainly there is no hint of anything like forced labour in Plutarch's own description of the variety of work done and the speed and enthusiasm with which it was completed. He was fortunate enough in having been able to see much more than we can see today, but a modern visitor to the Acropolis will still feel that unique quality of freshness and antiquity, of grace and of solidity, which so moved Plutarch nearly nineteen centuries ago and which, according to him, moved the contemporaries of Pericles in the same way. His account of the actual building and of the effect made by the completed work is as follows:[1]

> The materials used were stone, bronze, ivory, gold, ebony and cypress-wood; and the artists and craftsmen employed on shaping and working them were carpenters, moulders, bronze-smiths, masons, dyers, workers in gold and ivory, painters, embroiderers and workers in relief. Then there were those who dealt with the transport of the material – on sea, merchants and sailors and pilots, and on land, waggon-makers, owners of teams of draught animals, carters, rope makers, weavers, leather-workers, road-builders, and miners. And each art, like a general with his separate command, had its own throng of unskilled labourers organised to act in a subordinate capacity, like an instrument in the hands of a musician or a body under the control of the soul. There was employment for almost every age and almost every type of person and prosperity spread far and wide.
>
> And so the works rose up, stupendous in size and inimitable in the grace of their proportions; and the workmen vied with each other to excel in the beauty of their handiwork. But what was the most amazing thing about them was the speed with which they were done. People thought that each single one of them would have taken generations of workers to finish; and yet all of them were completed in the great years of just one administration . . . And this is why the works of Pericles are particularly amazing: they were done in such a short time to last for so long. Each one of them was, in its beauty, from the moment of its creation antique; yet in its bloom and freshness it is still at the present day something new and suddenly revealed. They glow with a kind of modernity which makes them look for ever beyond the reach of time, as though they were touched with an everlasting bloom and interfused with a spirit of agelessness.

The buildings which Plutarch mentions by name are the Parthenon, the sanctuary of the mysteries at Eleusis, the long wall connecting Athens with Piraeus, the Odeum and the Propylaea. Other temples dating from the same period are the temple of Hephaestus in Athens and the temple of Poseidon at Sounium. Of the Odeum we know little except what Plutarch tells us. It was a hall designed for the holding of contests

[1]*Lives*, 'Pericles', XII and XIII

Looking north-west across the interior of the Parthenon

in music, which were a part of the Panathenaic festival. According to Plutarch its interior contained many pillars and many tiers of seats and the circular, domed and tent-shaped roof was an exact reproduction of the Great King's pavilion. Vitruvius adds that part of the decoration consisted of the masts and spars of ships captured from the Persians.

The general overseer of all the works was Pericles' friend, the sculptor Phidias, though for the separate buildings different artists and architects were employed. The architects of the Parthenon, for instance, were Callicrates and Ictinus. The Propylaea was the work of Mnesicles.

One of the engaging qualities of Plutarch is that he has the modern liking for gossip; even though he strongly disapproves of scurrilous stories told about great men, he does not hesitate to repeat them. And in Pericles' own day the Athenians evidently loved gossip and political lampoons at least as much as they do now and had a great deal more freedom to express their feelings than has ever existed before or since. There was, for instance, the story that Phidias, on the pretext of showing well-born ladies round the new works of art, was in fact making assignations with them for his friend Pericles. Another of Pericles' friends, Pyrilampes, apparently had a collection of peacocks and was supposed to have allowed Pericles to use these birds as an irresistible bribe for women whom he was anxious to seduce. Plutarch, no doubt rightly, does not believe these stories; but, when he characterises their authors as men of disreputable life who gratify the envy of 'the many' by making fun of their betters, he is not writing like an Athenian.

One quotation which he gives from the comic poet Cratinus, the elder contemporary of Aristophanes and a man who did, indeed, have the reputation of a drunkard, is interesting in giving us a glimpse of how Pericles might have appeared to a caricaturist. He was writing, presumably, soon after the ostracism of Thucydides, the son of Melesias, and is making fun not only of the new building of the Odeum but also of Pericles' majestic manner (one nickname for him was 'the Olympian') and of the shape of his head, which was said to be like that of a squill and to have caused Pericles such embarrassment that he would never be portrayed in sculpture unless with a helmet on. The same kind of joke was made about Julius Caesar and his baldness. Cratinus writes:

> Now that the ostracism's done
> Our onion-headed Zeus appears
> With the Odeum stuck on his head
> Like a cap about his ears.

In another comedy Cratinus complains of the time being taken over the building of the Long Wall to Piraeus. Here he seems certainly to have been unjust. So far as most of the buildings were concerned, we know that, as Plutarch says, they were put up with almost incredible speed. The Parthenon, according to the building inscriptions, was completed in nine years (447/6–438) although the sculptures took another six years. The Propylaea were finished in five years (437–432). The Erechtheum

The Parthenon from the shadow of the Propylaea

(421–406) was begun after Pericles' death and all the building was done in war-time.

It would seem, therefore, that, whatever the comic poets might say, the Athenians showed their natural energy and '*philotimia*' or 'love of distinction' in performance of the work. Plutarch[1] tells a delightful story indicating that even the animals employed on the heavy labour shared in the general enthusiasm. He relates that during the building of the Parthenon there was at least one mule who showed a remarkable sense of honour:

> Every day, of course, great numbers of draught animals were used to bring up the stone, and of the mules there was one who had worked most nobly, but was discharged in the end because of old age. This mule used to go down every day to the Cerameicus and meet the other animals which were carrying up the stones. He would turn back with them and trot along at their side, as though urging them on and spurring them to greater effort. So the people of Athens, in admiration for its fine sense of honour and enterprise, ordered that it should be fed at the public's expense and voted it free meals, as for an athlete who had retired through old age.

The honours so deservedly bestowed on this mule were withheld from the great master-designer of the works, Phidias. By this time Pericles himself seems to have been in an unassailable position. Whatever jokes the comic poets might make about him, he was in fact generally respected and influential. His reputation for integrity was too high for there to be any chance of success for any attacks made on him in the law courts by his enemies on the common charges of bribery or malversation of the public funds. It was still possible to attack him indirectly by bringing charges against his friends, and this is what his enemies did. His old friend and tutor, the philosopher Anaxagoras, was accused of impiety and went into voluntary exile rather than face a trial. Another friend, the musician and musical theorist Damon, was ostracised. And Phidias was accused not only of impiety but embezzlement. The latter charge was easy to disprove, since the gold used on the gold and ivory statue of Athena was detachable and could be weighed, a procedure which showed that Phidias had taken none of it for himself; but the charge of impiety stuck and he also went into exile, spending the next years in constructing his other great gold and ivory statue, that of Zeus at Olympia.

The fact that these accusations of impiety could at such a time have such an effect is certainly surprising. It was an age of extraordinary freedom of thought and, as a rule, freedom from prejudice. Moreover, until the outbreak of the plague in Athens, it was an age of almost continual success. Particularly in the years during which the Parthenon was built there had been no serious setbacks or calamities which could have been fastened upon by the superstitious as evidence that the gods were displeased at the way things were going. Later, after the defeat of Athens and after the short period during which the city was governed by the Thirty Tyrants, some slight justification might be found in attacks on the new learning. Those members of the restored democracy who prosecuted Socrates for impiety and for corrupting the

[1]*Moralia*, 970

The frieze of the Parthenon shows a solemn procession of Athenians to the great four-yearly feast to the goddess of the citadel. Here, on the East Frieze, Artemis is casually pulling at her slipping garment as she sits watching.

youth could at least point to the celebrated and favoured disciples of the philosopher – Alcibiades, who had joined Sparta in the war against his own country, and Critias, who had been the leading and most cynically ruthless spirit among the Thirty. But no one could conceivably have charged any of the men in Pericles' circle with a lack of patriotism or with anti-democratic sentiment.

It remains true that even in the years of prosperity and of the enlightenment, when almost any idea or convention could be freely challenged and debated, juries could always be found to react fiercely to accusations of impiety. It seems almost as though the Athenians were capable at the same time of welcoming with enthusiasm and of rejecting with horror what was new and unconventional. Often we find what we should call 'sacred subjects' treated by the same author in the same play both with

The East Frieze of the Parthenon showing Poseidon, Apollo and Artemis. A detail is shown on page 116.

the deepest reverence and what would appear to be an unbecoming levity. In Aristophanes' *Frogs*, for instance, the chorus of those who have been initiated in the mysteries is reverent and god-fearing, while the god Dionysus is for much of the time a figure of fun. It has been pointed out that a somewhat similar mixture of religious feeling and of knockabout fun can be found in the miracle plays of the Middle Ages; but, since in all other respects the political and religious climates of the periods were so different, the parallel seems to indicate little more than the obvious fact that human beings can sometimes laugh at things which they can also take seriously. In ancient Greece there was no defined religious dogma and consequently no heresy.

There was certainly, however, impiety and it could be visited with severe penalties. But it is far from easy to see how the word was understood. The piety required of

Eastern view of the Parthenon

OVERLEAF: *North Frieze of the Parthenon. Part of the mounted procession*

an Athenian was not very like that of Aeneas and was very unlike that of a Victorian clergyman. Apart from the fact already noticed that no one seems to have objected to the telling of stories which made the gods look ludicrous, we actually find that the gods are often represented not only as ludicrous, but as unjust or even, by human standards, positively bad. Aeschylus and Pindar certainly did their best to put moral meaning into the old and often immoral stories; but they are lonely, if popular, figures in the fifth century, and, after the time of Aeschylus, no Athenian thinker, except, if we can believe Plato, Socrates, can be found to conclude unreservedly that the gods are good and just; and even Socrates does not pretend to know quite what they are doing. One may say, perhaps, that to be a proclaimed atheist was generally shocking; yet the complete metaphysical scepticism of the sophists is often scarcely distinguishable from atheism. Gorgias of Leontini, for instance, wrote a treatise in which he maintained, I, that nothing exists, II, that if anything does exist, it cannot be known, III, that if it can be known, the knowledge cannot be communicated by language. And Gorgias was greatly admired in Athens and even, in Plato's dialogue, is treated with politeness and considerable respect by Socrates himself. In an age in which radical speculation was, on the whole, so applauded, it seems odd that Anaxagoras should have been forced into exile. His impiety apparently consisted in teaching that the sun was a red-hot stone and that the moon was made of earth, and it is hard to believe that anyone could have regarded this doctrine as particularly dangerous thinking. Nor is it a very convincing explanation to say that the fickle Athenians had simply got tired of hearing Anaxagoras referred to as 'Old Intellect', on the analogy of the voter at the time of the ostracism of Aristides who, when asked what he had against this good man, is said to have replied, 'I'm just tired of always hearing him called "the Just".'

One may diffidently suggest that in all these trials for impiety politics played a greater part than religion. In the case of Anaxagoras the charge of impiety was coupled with a charge (almost certainly unjustified) of being pro-Persian. Phidias, as we have seen, was acquitted of the charge of embezzlement; and his impiety consisted not of any anti-religious sentiment, but of using his position to glorify Pericles and himself. According to Plutarch the shield of the statue of Athene was ornamented with a sculptured scene of a battle with the Amazons and in this scene Phidias had made a likeness of himself as an old man lifting up a stone and another of Pericles fighting with an Amazon (page 137). The figures were of men, not of gods; so it would be impossible that Phidias was representing either Pericles or himself as divine. It is likely that what really offended public opinion was the Athenian insistence on the equality of rights of all citizens. It was felt that on a national monument no particular citizen, and especially no greatly distinguished citizen, should be given a prominence that was denied to others. In this instance what was meant by impiety seems to have been self-advertisement rather than blasphemy. That ordinary men could be represented in the company of gods without any suspicion of blasphemy is evident. In Aeschylus' *Eumenides* the gods themselves plead their cases before an Athenian court of law, and in the Parthenon frieze Athenian men and

South Frieze of the Parthenon. Cattle on the way to the sacrifice

women move naturally and freely among the gods who share in their festival. And though these figures are said to be idealised in the manner of Phidias, it is at least likely that some of them were modelled on living Athenians. No one objected to this, perhaps because in none of the recognisable figures was there a likeness of any statesman or friend in Pericles' own circle.

Indeed all the evidence we have points to the fact that in later antiquity Phidias was regarded as pre-eminently the religious sculptor of the period. Cicero, Pausanias and Quintilian all agree that, particularly in the great gold and ivory figures of Athena in the Parthenon (page 136) and of Zeus at Olympia (page 145), the sculptor embodied in material form the highest and most sublime intuition of divinity. According to Quintilian[1] his Zeus actually added something to traditional religion, so majestic was it and so fitting to the nature of the divine.

Unfortunately nothing of his most famous work survives and it is difficult for us even to imagine at all clearly what such unfamiliar structures would look like to a modern eye. Of the majesty to which all who write of them bear witness we may form some conception from some works in stone or bronze which we still have – from the bronze figure of Zeus dragged up from the sea at Artemisium, for example, or from the Apollo from the pediment in Olympia, and best of all, perhaps, from the occasional quick pictures which Homer gives us of gods appearing in their full beauty, force and resistless strength – of Zeus nodding his head to Thetis and making the peaks of Olympus shake, of Apollo with his clanging arrows striding down from the mountain tops to the Greek camp, or of Poseidon going with gigantic steps across the sea.

Phidias may well in his gold and ivory statues have evoked the same feelings of awe as we feel in the presence of these earlier productions. But from the surviving sculpture of the Parthenon, which he planned and may in part have executed, this is not precisely the impression which we receive. In the pediments, the metopes and the frieze the gods are indeed represented as majestic, but the majesty is combined with a kind of human grace. The Zeus of Artemisium and the Apollo of Olympia are, in their human forms, supernatural powers, as are sometimes, though by no means always, the gods of Homer. But the gods of the sculptures on the Parthenon are not, for all their grace and majesty, altogether out of this world. They show a refinement of technical skill unequalled in the earlier works and a combination of grace and strength which has been unsurpassed. They are god-like certainly, but they are also remarkably like other statues of Athenian youths and athletes who make no pretensions, except for their beauty and their perfect physique, to divinity. One does not have to be a Hebrew prophet in order to recognise that in these graven images the distinction between the human and the divine is so slight as to be scarcely evident. The Theseus from the east pediment could just as well be a Hermes or an Apollo, and the deities in the frieze could just as easily be figures of their worshippers.

A religious thinker who is concerned to emphasise the remoteness of God from man, or to contrast the holiness of God with man's sinful and perverse state rather

[1]Inst. Orat. XII, 10, 9

North Frieze of the Parthenon. Boys carrying water. On the right one, who has been resting, stoops to replace his jar.

OVERLEAF: *The Caryatids on the porch of the Erechtheum*

than to suggest any possible likeness or even identity between the two, might with reason accuse Phidias and his fellow workmen of impiety. But he would find no support from the Greeks of antiquity. When Phidias makes his gods very like Athenians and his Athenians very like gods, he is working within the time-honoured and revered tradition of Homer himself. For though Homer at times presents us with pictures of the gods in tremendous and awe-inspiring aspects, they are never wholly inhuman and are often delightfully and even scandalously like men. Aphrodite can be shown, as in the scene in the *Iliad* where Helen attempts to revolt from her, as the irresistible and terrible force behind the love which controls men and gods alike, but she also makes a very poor showing on the battlefield and a somewhat disreputable one when she is trapped in bed with Ares by her wronged husband, Hephaistos. Later moralists, such as Plato, would be shocked by such presentations and would expurgate them from education in his Republic; and long before Plato philosophers had protested against the anthropomorphism of the poets and of popular belief. But the many Greeks who were not pre-eminently moralists or philosophers seem always to have been delighted with the thought of a certain friendly intimacy which might exist, and which in the age of the heroes certainly had existed, between the gods and men. Even a sophist at a much later date, when confronted by a sceptical young man who asked him, 'If the gods speak, what language do they use?' found himself constrained to reply, 'Either Greek or something very like it.'

Perhaps the nearest parallel which can be found to Phidias' intimate representation of the gods is in Homer's treatment of Athena in her relation to her two human favourites, Diomedes and, in particular, Odysseus. For Odysseus she feels an almost maternal tenderness which is combined with genuine admiration for his intelligence and his resolution; and Odysseus, while never lacking in respect to her, can usually see through her disguises and is not afraid to ask her why, in spite of her professed care for him, she has apparently done very little to help him through all the long years of his wanderings.

Athena, as might be expected, has the place of honour in the sculptures of the Parthenon. There was not only the colossal statue of her in gold and ivory in the cella of the temple, but she is also the main figure in both the groups of statuary which fill the pediments. That on the east shows her birth and that on the west her contest with Poseidon for the overlordship of Athens. And the inner frieze is devoted to the Panathenaic procession held in her honour.

The drawings done by J. Carrey in 1674, ten years before the explosion of a powder magazine inside the Parthenon during the Turkish-Venetian war had destroyed so much, indicate that even at that date the sculptures of the pediments were in a fair state of preservation. Most of what remained of them was brought to England in 1806 by Lord Elgin, who for this action was bitterly attacked by the greatest of the English phil-Hellenes, Lord Byron, in his poem *The Curse of Minerva*. Conveniently forgetting his own Scottish ancestry, Byron stigmatises Attila and Lord Elgin, whom he brackets together as 'the Gothic monarch and the Pictish peer', as the leading barbarous despoilers of the sacred city of Athens. Here he is perhaps somewhat

Poseidon, god of water and earthquakes. Though he was much revered, his rough character did not evolve to suit new theological ideas, partly because they tended to monotheism so that Zeus left little room for others, and his influence declined with the century.

unfair. The Romans were much greater predators, and Lord Elgin could certainly plead in his defence that, if the marbles were not in the British Museum, they would undoubtedly have gone within a few years to a museum in Germany. Today, however, when Athens contains so many and such distinguished archaeologists and shows a care for her ancient monuments which was not evident in the time of Lord Elgin, there are many modern English phil-Hellenes who would welcome a restoration of the lost property to its rightful owners and at the same time would be glad of the opportunity of seeing these sculptures in the light and against the background for which they were designed. And it is hard to find any justification whatever for the removal some years later from Athens to the British Museum of one single caryatid from the porch of the Erechtheum. Whatever one may think of the whole conception of this Porch of the Maidens, which was not the work of Phidias, it is impossible to find much pleasure in the sight of one solitary girl, strangely upright, with a weight of wholly meaningless marble resting unaccountably upon her head. She would at least have some meaning and a curious beauty where she belongs.

The separation of so much of Greek sculpture of this period from the environment for which it was designed may account for some, at least, of the critical judgments made upon it. When, in discussing the work of Phidias, we use such terms as 'naturalism' or 'idealisation' (and Phidias has been both admired and reproached for each of the two), we may be artificially both isolating and generalising about the objects in front of our eyes. Sculptures and bronzes in the usually subdued light and in the modern surroundings of a museum cannot, without some effort of the imagination, be considered as anything but 'objects of art'. When we look at them, we tend, as with so much else, to analyse rather than to enjoy or to revere; we may admire the technical skill shown in treatment of drapery or applaud the Greek knowledge or discovery of the laws of proportion. Greek thinkers both before and after Phidias attempted what may be the impossible task of explaining art in terms of abstract ideas. The importance of proportion was recognised by the artists themselves and the laws of proportion, so far as they could be expressed mathematically, were carried over from art and music into metaphysics by Pythagoras and later by Plato and were invested with a religious solemnity. The universe itself, according to Plato, is constructed on geometrical proportions. Such a notion may, in the eyes of metaphysicians, confer a kind of dignity on art, although, as we shall see, Plato himself, great artist as he was, took the opposite view, dismissing most art as the imitation of an imitation of reality. However, valuable as these metaphysical theorisings may be, they do not seem greatly to have affected the practice of artists in the age of Phidias, who were more concerned to emphasise the continuity between the seen and the unseen than any dichotomy between the two.

Maurice Bowra, in an admirable chapter of his book *The Greek Experience*, writes as follows on this subject:

'It was this sense of a connexion between the seen and the unseen, between the

[1]*The Greek Experience*, C. M. Bowra, Chapter VIII, 'The Plastic Vision'. London, Weidenfeld and Nicolson, New York, The World Publishing Company, 1957

accidental and the essential, between the transitory and the permanent, which provided Greek art with a guiding ideal and a welcome discipline and ennobled it with an exalted detachment and a consistent, self-contained harmony.

'This outlook made Greek art what it is and accounts alike for its special qualities and for the lack of much that we like and admire in the art of other peoples. In its archaic and classical periods its most marked characteristic is that, though it is always concerned with the search for beauty, it makes this familiar and at home in its presentation of it. There is nothing alien or violent or unapproachable in its visions of gods and heroes. They are related to the known world and, even if they are nobler than anything in it, they have somehow a place in it and seem to belong to it. So far from making us feel that there is a gap between things as we see them and as they really are, Greek art insists that they are one, that each stresses the nature of the other in a single unity, which reflects a complete and single world.'[1]

This view of 'a complete and single world' does not imply any blurring of distinction. No doubt the artists were as aware of the contrast between the One and the Many or the seen and the unseen as were the philosophers and poets of the period. But, as Bowra indicates, their aim was a harmony in which the different elements of which it is composed are recognised as real, but not seen as conflicting or incongruous. Only if the representation of such a world is, in some sense, irreligious, can Phidias rightly be convicted of impiety.

This reclining figure on the east pediment of the Parthenon has been variously identified as Theseus (a hero), Herakles (a hero, but sometimes worshipped) and Dionysus (a god), illustrating how nearly identical gods and humans had become.

SOPHOCLES

The sculpture of Phidias has very often been taken together with the poetry of Sophocles as being typical of the classic outlook of the fifth century at its best. What is particularly admired and particularly regarded as typical is the balance, the harmony, the control and the serenity of both artists. And there is, of course, much truth in this conventional view. But it is a truth which, though obvious at a great distance, is, especially in the case of Sophocles, extremely difficult to approach closely or to hold in the tight and too often distorting grip of critical analysis.

A rather touching quality shared by many critics is to be found in their belief that the author should conform to their critical apparatus rather than that they should adapt it to the work which they are attempting to elucidate. The most glaring example, of course, is in the great Dr Johnson's entire approval, on moral and critical grounds, of Nahum Tate's restoration of *King Lear*, so that the innocent Cordelia should not only be saved from death but should reward the good Edgar with her hand in marriage. But Sophocles too has suffered from the pious Aristotelians; an almost incredible amount of ingenuity has been expended in discovering sin, *hubris* or at least a tragic flaw in the character of Oedipus, even although no spectator in the theatre and no reasonably sane judge of character can possibly find any fault in him except a rather quick temper which is, under the circumstances, not at all discreditable.

The fact is that, if we understand Aristotle's word '*hamartia*' as meaning 'a moral fault in the character of a man otherwise noble', this formula, while it would fit in well with the character of Macbeth, is simply not applicable to the Oedipus whom we see in Sophocles. On some modern critics this fact has dawned, but often they seem so shocked by the discovery that, instead of wondering whether Aristotle may have meant something else, they hurry feverishly and sometimes with great skill to repair the damaged fabric with some other all-inclusive formula of their own invention. They are strangely unhappy at the prospect of having to confront a variety of tragedies or of tragic heroes. Nothing will content them except *the* tragic hero or *the* tragedy. One sometimes wonders whether they would be really pleased if they were

Sophocles, said to have composed 123 plays, won 24 victories, each for a set of three tragedies and a satire, making 96 plays judged to be successes; in other contests he was placed second, but never third. Eight survive.

to succeed in constructing a philosophic model of the tragedy so perfect and accurate as to make it for the future unnecessary ever to visit the theatre or to read or write a play.

As we have seen, the word 'typical' is a difficult and dangerous word to use with regard to almost every aspect of Greek life, and as for what the Greeks themselves called 'tragedies', about the only elements common to all of them are to be found in the formal and conventional structure of prologue, choruses and episodes. The plays do not even always have unhappy endings, nor do they all have a hero. And the differences exist not only among the authors but within the works of the same author. Aeschylus' Prometheus can certainly be called the hero of the play which bears his name; but who is the hero of the *Oresteia*? Some plays of Sophocles – the *Oedipus Tyrannus* and the *Women of Trachis* for instance – end in what can appear to be a total defeat of virtue and good intentions which must have shocked Dr Johnson at least as much as Shakespeare's ending of *King Lear*. In other plays, such as the *Philoctetes* and the *Oedipus at Colonus*, virtue is wholly and unexpectedly rewarded. Euripides has been described by distinguished scholars both as 'the Rationalist' and 'the Irrationalist'. Some of his plays, like the *Helen*, which is a romantic escape story, are scarcely even serious; and, to make matters worse, it is Euripides whom Aristotle describes as 'the most tragic of the poets'.

Still the brave critics sally out, as it were in the quest of some holy grail, to discover a single formula, a single meaning or intention, under which they can subsume so much variety and even so much seeming inconsistency. Some come to sad, and even ridiculous, ends, and among these are the ones who aim at explaining everything in terms of the latest textbooks on psychoanalysis or anthropology. Some in the course of their quest have fascinating and enlightening adventures. Others, among whom are some of the very humblest knights, actually achieve their object and discover that it was there all the time in front of their eyes and at the point from which they began. What made it so difficult to see was only that they were looking for something else. The holy grail of their imaginations never existed. There is no single formula, religious, philosophical, aesthetic, psychological or neo-critical which can be expressed in prose to explain everything. But instead there is something much more splendid and impressive – a living harmony made up of divergencies, a truth, not of prose but poetry, a measure, again to adapt the words of Pericles, where rest and action, reality and imagination, move hand in hand.

This is not to suggest that all the plays of Sophocles, or of anyone else, have the kind of perfection which we ascribe to divinity. But in considering them we are wise to follow the lead of such scholars as Kitto who base their criticism on the assumption that the three great Greek dramatists knew perfectly well what they were doing, and are likely to have been at least as intelligent as a modern critic and may well have been more so. The assumption may seem obvious, indeed self-evident. Unfortunately it is not generally shared.

And even the most becoming reverence for an author may still lead us to attribute to him virtues which we have admired in others and which we think necessary to the kind of greatness which we want to admire. It may be, for example, that that great and wise scholar, Gilbert Murray, so loved and admired both Euripides and Swinburne and William Morris that he came to what now seems to us the odd conclusion that the Greek poet should be represented in English in a style modelled on that of those two late Victorians. Or, if we appreciate the real seriousness of the Greek tragedians, we may assume that true seriousness must imply in the poet a monotheistic or even a biblical or proto-Christian outlook on things. So the Middle Ages made Virgil into a prophet of the birth of Christ and so, in more modern times, the Athenian untranslatable *kaloskagathos* has been equated with the idea of the English gentleman.

Further examination will show, of course, that these pious approximations are inappropriate. The Greek poets were not theologians; Virgil's Augustus was not at all like Christ; and a *kaloskagathos* like Alcibiades would probably have been expelled from any good English public school before he had completed a term. But we shall be much more wildly wrong than any reverent Victorian if we proceed to say that the Greek poets were not serious or not concerned with the gods, that Virgil was not impressed by human suffering or that that *kaloskagathos* had no gentlemanly qualities. The last and most hopeless circle of whatever hell may be provided for critics is occupied by those who, having recognised the great difficulty there is in finding a single and easily stated meaning or intention in a work of art, conclude that they are at liberty to give to it any meaning which they like. Such lost souls are often to be found among modern producers of Shakespeare.

The classical scholars who have attempted to elucidate Sophocles have, to do them and their discipline justice, seldom proved themselves so totally irresponsible as have those Shakespearean producers who have attempted to show us, for example, that *Othello* can best be understood on the assumption of a homosexual relationship between the leading character and Iago. The critics of Sophocles do, as a rule, agree that he means something and that whatever meaning they find must be supported by the text and the action of the plays. And very often their various interpretations are not so wholly different from each other as the critics themselves appear to think. Those who hold what may be called the conventional view of Sophocles will lay stress on the harmony and serenity of his work and the piety, or *sophrosyne*, of the poet. They find that he shows us a world in which man, when confronted with the gods, is helpless. It is his duty and his wisdom to submit to the will of heaven. To challenge this will is both impious and futile and man will find his greatness in a dignified resignation to it.

Others, including some excellent critics of our own day, will maintain that serenity is not what we find in Sophocles, that, on the contrary, the typical (unfortunate word) Sophoclean hero is marked not by resignation, but by self-assertion and a violent intransigence. In his world the good will suffer not for their faults, but for their goodness, which is often expressed in acts of rebellion, as in the cases of Antigone, who refuses to obey a lawful authority, and Oedipus, who does everything in his power to make the oracle not come true. What Sophocles is emphasising is not the

*Two statuettes copied from the
colossal gold and ivory Athena
Parthenos of Phidias. LEFT:
an unfinished Roman version
includes the decoration on her shield.
RIGHT: also Roman, A.D. 130,
the most accurate copy in existence
but mechanically executed.*

power of the gods so much as the greatness of man. Nor is serenity a word that can be used of his supernatural world. For instance his play *The Women of Trachis* ends in the frustration of every good intention; in the death by slow and extreme torture of the great hero, Heracles, with no hope (which could easily have been given) of any ultimate reward; and the words, 'There is nothing in all this which is not Zeus'.

Yet other critics, possibly torn between these two views and also, perhaps, recognising that there is something to be said for each of them, get rid of what they see as a dilemma by suggesting that after all Sophocles was not interested in such problems. His main concern was to make a credible, fast-moving and exciting play or piece of theatre and he secured his effects by means of clear-cut characters and situations, recognitions, reversals of fortune and the rest, all done with an amazing dexterity and technical brilliance. The ideological aspects of his work, so far as they are important at all, are so only because of their relevance to the shaping of the stage characters and to the movement of the plot.

This view of Sophocles as a supreme puppet-master and nothing else need not detain us long. It is discredited by the experience of everyone who has ever seen or read a play of Sophocles; nor would a dramatist who seemed to have nothing valuable, in a political, moral or religious sense, have ever managed to get a play produced in Athens during the fifth century, let alone have so constantly have been awarded the first prize. We can applaud Sophocles' unquestionable technical proficiency without maintaining that such proficiency is best exercised in a moral and intellectual vacuum.

As for the other two views mentioned above, they are not irreconcilable, so long as neither of them is absurdly exaggerated. If we interpret the conventional serenity of Sophocles to mean that his is a world full of sweetness and light rather like that which Dickens may have believed awaited in a future state the spirit of Little Nell, we shall of course be guilty of absurdity. But it is no less absurd to maintain that the typical Sophoclean hero is determined to destroy himself and is somehow doing this to spite the gods and for the greater glory of man. All heroes, whether in Homer or Sophocles or anywhere else, are prepared to face death rather than dishonour. But this does not mean that they are determined to die before their time. The hero, also, is of course concerned with his own honour and will react to insult or injury in a way which may often bring him into conflict with authority, as happened in the quarrel between Achilles and Agamemnon. But this does not mean that his pride is such that he will acknowledge nothing greater than himself. At the height of his anger with Agamemnon, Achilles is still able to control himself when faced with the intervention of Athena. He is invariably respectful to the gods and knows the limitations of his human condition. There is indeed one occasion, and one only, when he actually opposes a very minor deity, the river god Xanthus, and in the fight which follows he has very much the worst of things. Those who select Achilles as a prototype of their typical Sophoclean hero – aggressive, intransigent, assertive against gods and men – have indeed chosen a most unfortunate example. No one is more aware than Achilles of his own ultimate helplessness.

Roman copy of the shield of Phidias' Athena Parthenos. The bald Greek on the left about to strike a fallen Amazon is said to be Phidias himself and the helmeted man beside him whose arm hides his face, Pericles.

OVERLEAF: *The miraculous birth of Aphrodite from the sea, or simply a woman emerging from her bath.*

No one also is more aware of his own genuine strength and of his own dignity. And it seems true that much of the difficulties and diversities we find among critics may come from the error of their assumption that to believe in the superior powers of the gods must imply a belief in the total impotence and worthlessness of man. This assumption has indeed been made by some philosophers and religious thinkers. It is quite evidently not made by Homer or by any writers of the fifth century. Sophocles and Homer are alike aware of the great gulf fixed between any man, even a hero, and the gods; but they are also aware of something in common. Men too can be, if only briefly and at certain moments, god-like; but they will not be god-like unless they are also conscious of their limitations. The mortal hero may be, for a brief moment, lit up with the same brightness in which the gods are always illuminated and there are degrees of the peculiar excellence which they may attain. But the ray of brightness cannot last; it can only be remembered. This, of course, does not mean that it is without value. In the Homeric world and, in a rather, but not wholly, different sense, in the world of Pericles, it is much more valuable than anything else.

Sophocles himself is said to have claimed that in his plays he represented men 'as they should be', whereas Euripides showed them 'as they are'. And much the same distinction might be made between the sculpture of Phidias and that of the Hellenistic period. But here the use of such words as 'idealism' and 'realism' may prove to be misleading. There is nothing shadowy or insubstantial about Phidias' sculpture or Sophocles' characters. What particularly strikes one is their solidity. In contrast it is the characters of Euripides and the later sculpture which often show an exaggeration, a fluidity and an uncertainty which, though undoubtedly to be found in real life, seem more impressionistic and less stable than the creations of the earlier artists.

In the Parthenon frieze the Athenians, young and old, men and women, do in the glad moment of their national celebration move naturally and effortlessly in the presence of the gods and to this extent may be said to have assumed divinity just as the gods have, for a moment, assumed humanity. Here the gods appear naturally in a social context with men. But when they are represented in action and in the exercise of power, they are different. The Zeus of Artemisium and also, according to all report, the colossal statues of Athena in the Parthenon and of Zeus at Olympia, are altogether superhuman in majesty, energy and power. In the extant plays of Sophocles the gods only very rarely appear on the stage, as they do often in Aeschylus and, even more frequently, in Euripides. And only in the very last play that Sophocles wrote, the *Oedipus at Colonus*, is there any clear indication of the hero actually entering, in some sense, into the company of the gods. Without doing any violence to the mythological material Sophocles might have rewarded the suffering Heracles in the same way at the end of the *Women of Trachis*; but he does nothing of the kind. On the whole the action of the human characters is perfectly self-explanatory and requires no divine intervention. It is true that Athena has caused the temporary madness of Ajax and that it was because of an oracle that Oedipus left what he imagined to be his home in Corinth. But these events have taken place before the actions of the plays begin.

The charioteer, with translucent onyx for the pupils of his eyes, was a revolutionary work. With the strong vertical line of his tunic, he was designed to be seen from below. See also page 160.

Everything that happens after this depends on the characters of the human beings concerned who are under no constraint to behave in any way other than that in which we imagine that they would behave normally. Whatever the circumstances may be in which the characters find themselves, the choices which they make are their own and even when they are to the audience horrifying, as with the self-blinding of Oedipus, they are still seen to be, in a sense, right.

It is for this reason, no doubt, that many admirers of Sophocles emphasise the certainty of his touch in the delineation of character and in the manipulation of plot. These virtues he most evidently possesses, but this is by no means a complete list of them. Though the gods do not appear in visible form with anything like the same frequency as in Aeschylus and in Euripides, and though the action can be regarded as self-explanatory in human terms, in fact the presence of the gods is throughout at least as evident to the audience in Sophocles as it is in the works of the other two dramatists, and the human action, while completely consistent with the development of the human characters represented, also is felt to follow a path which is parallel with a divine path and which inevitably must be so. It is quite certain that to Sophocles the gods exist and are powerful, that the actions of the men must conform to this superior power and that, though its precise workings may be inscrutable, it deserves our reverence.

This does not at all mean, it should not be necessary to say, that man is worthless, a mere puppet in the hands of totally alien forces. We shall never know what precisely was Sophocles' religious faith or even whether such a phrase is applicable. And if we say that he was pious or god-fearing, this does not mean that he was a pietist or a subscriber to any particular religious dogma. In his time there was no pietism nor anything which could be called dogma. Nor can he be called, except in the very broadest sense, a metaphysician. Such problems as free will and the origin of evil, if they presented themselves to him at all, did not do so in modern philosophical or theological terms.

Of his personal life, as of the personal lives of the other great writers of the fifth century, we know very little, though perhaps more than we know of the life of Shakespeare. He was skilled in music and poetry, good-looking, courteous and easy-going; on at least two important occasions he held high military and political office. Leaving his poetry aside, one must think of him as distinguished, but distinguished in a normal way. There were many others like him. Much the same may be said of Shakespeare, though Shakespeare, unlike Sophocles, never commanded a fleet. And in Shakespeare's case too what evidence there is suggests that his friends found him an agreeable companion, not in any way particularly odd, not noted for any metaphysic or for anything remarkably daring in the way of religious thought. Each of the two dramatists lived in a period of invention, discovery and tremendous intellectual ferment and it is evident from their works that they were both keenly aware of the tensions, paradoxes and conflicting theories of their times. So again were many other people. But these many others, who, while they might better 'abide our question' on particular points at issue in politics, metaphysics and religion, lack the supreme greatness which everyone finds in the poetry of Sophocles and Shakespeare. To the bewilderment of many, these great authors fail signally to come out with any obviously new or original doctrine. The mirrors which they hold up to nature reveal much blood, suffering, endurance and terror, much that is surprising or wholly unexpected. At the end of their plays we may be sobered, drained or even purged; we may not quite know where we are. Yet what we have seen has been no hallucination, in spite of the magic; the mirror has been held steadily and what we have been looking at has been, in fact, just like life. We may wish that Oedipus had never discovered the secret of his birth or, (as Dr Johnson did) that Cordelia had lived to marry Edgar; but in our hearts we know that things must have happened as they did and in our hearts we are, if not quite, as Yeats would have it, 'gay', at least content,

Phidias's colossal Zeus of Olympia in gold and ivory, the most admired statue of its age, is known to us only from this Roman copy (AD 133) of a Greek coin, c.340.

even, if one may dare to use the offending word, serene. And these moments at the end of a play, moments of awe, gaiety, content or serenity, simply do not leave scope for such speculations as 'What exactly was Oedipus' "tragic flaw"?' or 'Why did not Othello inquire from Emilia about the handkerchief?' The action as we have seen it is complete and such subsequent questions are usually found to be pointless. They would be natural to ask if we were reading a detective story; but we know that the detective story is not more life-like than the tragedy; it is simply more ordinary.

By 'ordinary' I mean that these lesser works of art, the real merits of which I should be the last to deny, are written in a convention of extreme simplicity, a convention which may be very useful to us in our everyday lives but which, in situations of real difficulty, we recognise to be misleading or of only limited value. In ordinary living and while reading a detective story we accept readily enough the assumptions that the policeman and the detective have a certain dignity as guardians of the law and instruments for bringing the criminal to justice. The law is assumed to be good and its agents are often presented as more attractive than they usually appear in real life.

The criminal is assumed to be bad and, if he can be represented, as Dr Moriarty was, as a veritable 'Napoleon of crime', we are all the better pleased. All the time we know that this is an absurd over-simplification. While in most cases we certainly deplore crime and approve obedience to the law, it is also evident that many good men have been condemned as criminals and that such a thing as police brutality does exist. But we do not allow our knowledge of these obvious facts to spoil our enjoyment of a clever plot with its appropriate decoration. We enjoy the blood from which we would shrink in real life and we applaud in the detective an intelligence or virtue which reflection would show to be superhuman.

It is true that a fictional story in prose is capable of great fluidity and variation and that a writer such as Graham Greene is able, as it were, to have it both ways, to give us the excitement of the chase and still make us admire the criminal more than his pursuers. But this is rare and even Greene has to bring in 'the gods' in order to break through the comfortable convention.

The religious convention in which Sophocles and Shakespeare write is not comfortable. Not only do terrible things happen but we feel them to be terrible. Nor is there any easy solution to the moral problems involved. Antigone and Oedipus do not deserve their fates any more than do Juliet or Desdemona or Hamlet. Though there is a clear distinction between the good and the bad, it may often seem that this distinction is not important to the gods, or fate or heaven. Though it is often evident that people learn by suffering, this does not seem to be, as in Aeschylus, part of a divine plan. Usually they learn too late and the only people who can profit from the knowledge are the minor characters and the audience.

And yet these great plays, for all the unsolved questions that they raise, are satisfying. And a large part of our satisfaction comes from the fact that in the sequence and interplay of events and characters we see or feel the presence of a certain order even though it is beyond the scope of our philosophy. There are indeed more things in heaven and earth than we had imagined, but our very recognition of their existence is a valuable gain. The truth that is visible to us is bigger, more extensive and more powerful than is suggested by our common work-a-day beliefs, but it is neither fiendish nor chaotic. The greatness of man is not diminished by his knowledge of his mortality.

The Four Winds as dancing girls painted on a knucklebone, a popular game, though this one is too handsomely decorated to be thrown about

OVERLEAF: *The Temple of Poseidon at Sounium*

SOPHOCLES

HIS LAST PLAY

In considering Sophocles' last play, the *Oedipus at Colonus*, written just before the poet's death in his ninetieth year, it is not suggested that this work marks in any but a temporal sense a culmination of his art or provides any final answer to the questions which have vexed his critics. His long life (from 495 to 406), started five years before the battle of Marathon and ended one year before the Athenian fleet was destroyed at Aegospotami and two years before Athens was starved into surrender. He wrote more than a hundred plays and it is natural to suppose that in the course of writing them there must have been some kind of development in thought and in technique. However, if there was we are quite unable to trace it. Of his more than a hundred plays only seven survive and the earliest of these, the *Ajax*, was probably written when the poet was already in his fifties. Thus, as Bowra reminds us, 'what we have of his work comes from his mature years, and even when he wrote the *Ajax*, he may have been older than Shakespeare when he retired to silence and death at Stratford'.[1]

In all the extant plays we admire the perfection of style and of dramatic form. The criticisms which, in Aristophanes' *Frogs*, the imagined ghosts of Aeschylus and Euripides fling at each other are, we often feel, to some extent justified. The language of Aeschylus is at times exaggerated or bombastic; Euripides can be over-subtle or sentimental. But no such charges can be brought against Sophocles. His use of language is more subtle than that of Euripides, and, largely for this reason, he seems to be much the most difficult of the three tragedians to translate. But he is never just being clever; his control never wavers. His action is as grand as that of Aeschylus, though, within the bounds of a single play rather than of a trilogy, it is necessarily more rapid. But the grandeur, real as it is, is explicable in human terms, seen in a clear light rather than veiled in the mists of speculation or of monstrous, if magnificent, imagery.

And there are two other qualities which we find in all the plays. One, which has been well emphasised by such recent critics as Whitman and Knox, is the strange, almost superhuman, intransigence of the leading character. In this respect quite

[1]*Landmarks in Greek Literature*, p. 121, C. M. Bowra, London, Weidenfeld and Nicolson; New York, The World Publishing Company, 1955

Delphi, the supreme oracle of Greece and supposed centre of the (flat) earth. A young woman in a state of frenzy, characteristically gave a truthful answer so cryptic or uniformative as to be of no help—as when she told Oedipus his dreadful future but not who his parents were, so that he could successfully avoid them.

different protagonists, such as Antigone, Heracles, Oedipus and Philoctetes, are alike. Others may bow before the storm, but these heroes never give in. They have the dignity of a Prometheus and, in a sense, a dignity that is still greater than his, since, unlike him, they can not only feel agony but can die of it. Also they are not, as he is, fortified by any belief that they are in any way greater or better than the gods who may appear either to be crushing them or to have deserted them.

The other quality common to all the plays is the unexpectedness of the action or of the results of the action or of both. This is often expressed with a kind of irony which suggests that these great and often good characters are, in spite of or because of their very greatness and goodness, going naturally and inevitably in just the direction which, if they only knew the facts, they would either avoid or would face with horror. Yet in this irony there is no trace of bitterness and still less of cynicism. The characters may move blindly, but they never fail to arouse our admiration or respect. Even Creon, in the *Antigone*, who is not an admirable character, deserves our pity. He is also the only one who attempts, vainly and too late, to go back on the action which he has taken.

But though the intransigence of the leading characters and the irony, which includes pity and terror, with which their action is treated are evident in all the plays, the variety of both character and action is so great and the emphasis is so differently

The infant Oedipus, exposed on a mountain because Apollo had warned that he would kill his father, was saved by a shepherd.

RIGHT: *Oedipus and the Sphinx whose riddle he solved. She then killed herself and the grateful citizens made Oedipus ruler of Thebes.*

distributed in each of the plays, that even these fairly valid generalisations will seem sometimes incomplete or actually misleading. Antigone, for instance, in the play that bears her name, deliberately chooses her fate and we must believe that she would still have chosen it, even if she had been aware of all the consequences. Deianira, the loving wife of Heracles, in the *Women of Trachis* would have done anything rather than what she did do, could she only have known that in attempting to win back her husband's love she would be destroying him. And as character, emphasis and plot differ widely from play to play, so the same character is often very far from being the same in one play as he was in another. The Creon of the *Oedipus at Colonus* is a much worse man than he was in the *Antigone* or the *Oedipus Tyrannus*. The Odysseus of the *Ajax* is utterly different from the crooked political Odysseus who appears in the *Philoctetes*. The wholly confident and resolute young woman Antigone, in the play of that name, differs from the kind and selfless girl who is seen leading her blind father in the *Oedipus at Colonus*.

The prophet Tiresias is indeed exactly the same person in the two plays in which he appears, but his is not a complicated character; his role is simply that of the seer who brings from his supernatural knowledge extremely unwelcome information to the king at the height of his power. Of all the complex and heroic characters in Sophocles the only one fully to preserve his identity in two different plays is Oedipus.

Some thirty years after he had appeared in the *Oedipus Tyrannus*, in the height and vigour of his power and in his sudden, terrible and self-impelled disillusion, Sophocles in his last play returns to him and shows us exactly the same man at the very end of his life, altered only by time, suffering and infirmity, but with all the pride, passion and intellectual vigour that he ever had.

His inner strength and assurance are not shown at once. First we see on the stage an old, blind beggar with a girl leading him by the hand. In his opening words he identifies this girl as Antigone. He does not know to what land he has come; he is a wanderer, cityless, begging for his daily bread and getting little enough of it. Yet to him that little is enough; his sufferings have taught him to endure, as has the long time which has grown old with him and, finally, he has been instructed too by his genuine and innate nobility. He asks his daughter to find out where they are and if there is anywhere near where they can take refuge.

Antigone tells him that she can see in the distance the towers and walls of a city and this, she conjectures, must be Athens, since every traveller has told them that they are going in that direction. As for the place where they now are, it must be some sacred place; it is a grove where laurels, olives and vines are growing and from within it come bursts of song from the nightingales. She leads him to a rock where he can sit down while she makes further enquiries, but at this moment a stranger, one of the local inhabitants, is seen approaching.

When told that he is near, Oedipus addresses him politely, but has not said more than a few words when the stranger interrupts him and tells him to leave at once the place where he is sitting, since he is on holy ground. No one must set his foot in this grove; it is the home of the terrible children of Earth and Darkness, the Erinyes, who are invoked here by the name of the Eumenides, 'the Kindly Ones'.

Oedipus now speaks with assurance; he prays the goddesses to be kindly to him, their suppliant, since from this place he will never depart. The stranger, a law-abiding and kindly man himself, admits that he has no right to force the old man to move without the authority of the city and, in reply to further questions, tells him more about where he is. The place is rich in divinities. It is under the guardianship of Poseidon and close by is a shrine to Prometheus, the Fire-bearer; the hero Colonus is also honoured here and has given his name to the district, which is not especially well-known but is none the less dear to its inhabitants. Their ruler is the king of Athens, Theseus. Finally he agrees to send a message to the king, to whom the blind beggar promises a great gain in return for a little service.

Oedipus and Antigone are now alone and the old man prays again to the dread goddesses. Apollo, it appears, has told him that after years of suffering he will come in the end to a place where he will find rest and, in ending his life, will bring benefits to the land which receives him and curses to the land which has driven him out. There will be, so Apollo has said, signs given when this moment has come – earthquake or thunder or lightning. Now he recognises that the time is approaching and that the place will be here. He addresses his prayer to the goddesses and to Athens, 'most famous of cities'. May they pity this wretched shadow who was once Oedipus!

A seer from the pediment of the temple of Zeus at Olympia. Like Tiresias he forsees disaster, but is powerless to prevent it.

His prayer is only just finished when the chorus of old men of Colonus enter. They have heard that some foreigner has dared to set foot on the holy ground and, in an agitated lyric metre, they hunt for him like hounds on the trail.

When Oedipus shows himself, they insist that first of all he must come forward from the sacred place. They promise that, if he does so, no one will force him against his will to go further. He obeys them and Antigone leads him a little way forward and seats him again on a rock. Now that the chorus are satisfied they ask the usual questions: who is he? what is his country and who are his parents? Gradually and reluctantly Oedipus begins to tell them, but when they hear his name they start back from him in horror. He must leave the country at once, they say, or he will bring a curse on it; as for their promise not to drive him away, that is invalid; they had meant well to him, but he, by his very existence, can only repay their kindness with injury, the injury of his own pollution. They do indeed pity both him and his daughter, but they reverence the gods more and the gods have made clear what view they take of Oedipus.

At this point the old, blind and helpless beggar, with everyone against him, makes one of those speeches, full of authority and of intellectual force, which show us that he is still the naturally kingly man, still gifted with the same keen and irresistible logical power that he had in the days of his greatness. What good is there, he asks, in a great reputation and a famous name? Athens has been thought of as the most god-fearing of all cities, a place always ready to be a refuge for the afflicted. But what has he found? They have induced him to leave his sanctuary and are now driving him away. Yet how can they be afraid either of him or of what he has done? As for his deeds, he has suffered evil rather than done it. In his real nature no evil at all is to be found. 'I went where I went, not knowing where I was going.' No one knew except the gods, who were destroying him. And he sternly warns the chorus not to offend the gods by breaking their promise and by disgracing the good name of Athens. He himself has come among them as a god-fearing man who can do them good, and they shall hear more when their king has come to judge the matter.

The chorus are impressed by this dignified and strangely authoritative appeal. They, like their fellow-countryman earlier, are content to leave things alone until the chief power in the state has reached a decision.

And now a new character appears. A woman comes riding towards them and Antigone soon recognises her as her sister Ismene. She has ridden out to them from Thebes with one faithful servant with news of her brothers and Oedipus' sons, Eteocles and Polynices, who are equally hateful to Oedipus himself, since they have banished him and slighted him. All the kindness and care which he has received in his sufferings has come from his two daughters.

Now, as Ismene tells us, the brothers have quarrelled. At first they had been willing to leave the throne of Thebes to Creon, the brother of Jocasta, Oedipus' mother and wife, in the hope that by so doing they themselves would escape the curse which had already afflicted the two previous generations of their family. But this resolution did not last. Each of them wanted the kingship for himself and in the end the younger of the two, Eteocles, drove his brother Polynices into exile. Polynices has now gone to Argos where he is raising an army to attack his own native land. And there is further news which affects Oedipus himself. It has been learned from the oracle at Delphi that the old, blind and exiled king has a positive value. His presence, alive or dead, will bring power to those who have it near them.

Oedipus' comment, when he hears this, is:

> So when I cease to be, I then become a man.

And to Ismene's comforting assurance:

> The gods who once destroyed you raise you up again.

he replies:

> A little thing to raise up old who fell in youth!

Ismene goes on to say that Creon is already on his way to find Oedipus. It is not his intention to restore him to Thebes, but to place him under guard somewhere near the frontier, so that, when he dies, the Thebans will be in control of his tomb and have the benefit from it without risking any pollution by actually burying his body in Theban soil. Both brothers have heard the words of the oracle and both want to take advantage of it. Neither of them is willing to allow their father back into Thebes. What each wants is simply power for himself.

Oedipus denounces both of his sons and declares that nothing will make him leave the place where he now is. He recalls the distant past when, after the discovery of his identity, he had blinded himself and had begged for nothing better than to be stoned to death by his fellow citizens. But time passed and with time his anguish had grown less. He realised that he had already punished himself too severely for his involuntary guilt. It was then, years after the discovery, that he was driven out a beggar and an exile, and at that time his unnatural sons, a word from whom would have saved him, had done nothing to help him, while, unlike them, their sisters had given him everything they could give. But now, from these new oracles and from others known to him from the past, he is confident that he can resist Creon and all comers, so long as Athens and the dread goddesses protect him.

The chorus are impressed. They are now willing to do all they can for him; but first he must make the prescribed offerings to the goddesses into whose grove he has trespassed. His blindness incapacitates him from carrying out the ritual himself, but one of his daughters can act for him. Then, when Ismene has withdrawn into the grove to carry out the rites, the chorus again, in a lyrical dialogue, question Oedipus about his past. Can the terrible stories about him really be true?

Oedipus reluctantly and painfully submits to their questions. He has indeed killed his father, married his mother and begotten children who are at the same time his sons and daughters and his brothers and sisters. He himself feels all the horror at such things that the chorus feel; but again he vehemently protests his real innocence.

He killed a man in self-defence; he married a woman. It was impossible for him to have known that the man he killed was his father or that his wife was his mother.

Theseus now enters and in the scene which follows we immediately recognise a bond of likeness and of shared nobility between the two men. In his first speech Theseus expresses his sympathy with Oedipus and promises him the protection which he needs. He also was an exile, living in danger, in his youth; he knows that he is a man and that he can have no more certainty of what tomorrow will bring than has Oedipus himself. He makes no mention of the pollution which at first so terrified the chorus.

His generosity and understanding are such that it seems scarcely necessary for Oedipus to explain his present situation. One feels that even without the certain benefit which, still in somewhat mysterious terms, Oedipus promises will come to Athens if she provides him with his last resting place, Theseus would have welcomed him as a friend and a sufferer. In a fine speech, Oedipus points out that only the gods are immune from death and time; all else decays, hate turns to love and love to hate; now Theseus may have nothing to fear from Thebes, but a time will come when there will be war and a Theban army will be destroyed in the place where they now stand. Yet one feels that throughout all the changes and chances of time there is still something reliable and trustworthy in the friendship of these two men, both of whom can face good and bad alike without any diminution of their essential nobility.

Theseus offers Oedipus all and more than he has asked. He will make him a citizen of Athens and invites him to come back to the city with him, though leaving him free to live where he wills. Oedipus will stay where he is, at Colonus, since it is here, he feels, that he will conquer those who have thrown him out of his own land. So Theseus leaves the stage after once more promising his protection.

The chorus now sing an ode in praise of Colonus and, through Colonus, of Athens. This ode together with one in Euripides' *Medea* are the two most moving expressions in poetry of what it meant, in Pericles' words, to have 'fallen in love with' all that Athens stood for. But the ode of Euripides was written some thirty years before this one, at a time when Athens was at the height of her power. Now, in the old age of Sophocles, she is on the verge of utter collapse. Neither of the two poets in their glorious hymns of praise so much as mentions the empire or any specific achievement of the Athenians. Their emphasis is on Beauty, Wisdom, Love, the fruits of the earth and the presence of protecting gods. The ode of Sophocles begins, as the play itself began, with the nightingales singing continually in the shades of ivy in coverts on the sacred ground where Dionysus and the nymphs hold their revels. There also grow the narcissus and the crocus, wreaths from ancient times for the heads of the great goddesses, Demeter and Persephone. And next, in lines which must recall the ode of Euripides, who died just before the writing of this play, is mentioned the crystal stream of Cephissus where come the Muses and the Cyprian queen, Aphrodite.

The final strophes deal with the gifts, also commemorated on the Parthenon pediment, of the two protecting deities. There is the grey-leaved olive, which nourishes

A warrior leaving home

their youth, the gift of Athena, the grey-eyed goddess, who defends it for ever. And there are the gifts of Poseidon, the horse and the art of horsemanship, and the oar and the art of seamanship.

When Sophocles was writing this chorus the olive trees of Attica had been cut down and the crops burned year after year for more than a quarter of a century by invading Spartan armies; the invincible navy had already suffered appalling defeats and in the next year was to be utterly destroyed. But Sophocles' faith in and love for 'the real Athens' remains unaffected. It is not unlike the Athens of Aeschylus and, sometimes, of Euripides, the strong place where power and grace go together with reverence for the laws and for the gods, where authority is not oppressive or irresponsible and where freedom is not self-centred or chaotic. It is the same Athens as that which we see on the Parthenon frieze and sense behind the words of Pericles' funeral speech. It is hard indeed to say that it never existed.

There now occurs the first of two confrontations with his enemies which, as Oedipus dimly recognises, must precede his end. His wife's brother, Creon, who is in alliance with his son Eteocles, enters and attempts to persuade him to let him take him back to Thebes. This is a very different Creon from the Creon of the *Antigone*, which was written some forty years before. This Creon is smooth-tongued at first, deceitful, arrogant and, in the end, tyrannical.

The rather long scene which follows can be summarised briefly. Oedipus already knows that Creon's ostensibly kind offer to take him home to Thebes is a pretence, and that in fact the plan is to keep him under surveillance close to the frontier until he dies. He of course rejects the offer with scorn and finds that Creon's first words have already been belied in action. Creon's men have seized Ismene and now prepare to seize Antigone too. The old men of the chorus are horrified and prepare to defend Oedipus, but Antigone is forced away and carried off. At this point Theseus returns and immediately gives orders for a force of cavalry to ride in pursuit and rescue the two girls. Creon himself is placed under arrest. Theseus is outraged by the effrontery of Creon's action. He has come to a city which respects justice and does nothing without the authority of law and he is behaving like a common brigand. Does he imagine that Athens is a city without men or a city of slaves? That Theseus himself counts for nothing?

Creon now changes his tone completely. He has, of course, the greatest respect for Athens and for her king, but he simply could not believe that so god-fearing a city would harbour a polluted man like Oedipus. Incest and parricide are just the things that are most severely punished by the Athenian court of the Areopagus. Moreover Oedipus has incurred fresh guilt by calling down curses on the rulers of Thebes who themselves are perfectly friendly to Athens.

Oedipus answers with a more impassioned assertion of his real innocence than any that he has made so far. He has never willingly or knowingly committed any crime. And he comments scathingly on Creon's insensitivity and worse than bad taste in dragging again into the open the story of the incestuous marriage. Was not Oedipus' mother and wife Creon's own sister? Has she not suffered enough already?

The Charioteer, who has already won (he is wearing a victor's fillet), makes an offering to the gods. Though he is not a particular individual, his firm jaw and full, sensual lips show character, and, standing five feet eleven inches, he is a convincing sportsman.

*Oedipus in this version overcoming the Sphinx by force, his right foot on higher
ground. Apollo, seated on his mantle, watches from above.*

Theseus too is plainly disgusted by Creon's speech. He acts with the same speed
and energy as that with which Oedipus himself used to act in the days of his youth
and his power. Creon, vainly threatening, is forced to guide Theseus and his troops
on the way in their pursuit of the girls and their captors.

The old men of the chorus remain behind with Oedipus and in a vigorous song
speculate on the exploits of their king and his troops in their attempts to rescue the
prisoners. It soon appears that the expedition has been successful. Theseus returns
with Antigone and Ismene who are reunited with their father. His tenderness and
love for them will stand out in sharp contrast with the wholly unforgiving temper
which will mark his speeches to his son in the episode that follows.

It appears that on his way back from the rescue Theseus has encountered a stranger
who has begged leave to be allowed to speak to Oedipus. He claims some relationship and has, it seems, come from Argos. Oedipus recognises that this must be his
son, Polynices, who, driven from Thebes by his brother, has gone to Argos to raise
an army against those who have driven him out. At first Oedipus refuses to see his

ungrateful son whom he hates as much as he does Creon, but in response to pleas from Theseus and Antigone he consents to hear what the young man has to say.

This will be Oedipus' last trial; but before Polynices comes on the stage, the chorus sing that famous and terrible ode lamenting not only the miseries of old age but of life itself. Much the best thing is never to have been born; and the next best is to die as quickly as possible. Once youth has passed, there is nothing but a waste of sorrow and pain — envy, civil war, battle, strife and death by violence. Last and worst of all comes repulsive old age, without friends or companionship. All the old men feel this, but Oedipus himself is a crowning example of a man buffeted and rocked by blow after blow of misfortune. He stands like a rocky headland in a stormy sea with the storm winds bearing down upon him from east and west, north and south.

This is the picture that we have of the old Oedipus as he approaches the last and miraculous moments of his life on earth. It is useless to conjecture whether or not Sophocles may have been thinking of the contrast between his own brilliant youth in a city where, though there were plenty of battles, civil war was virtually unknown and friendship, companionship and optimism were in the air, and the time of his old age, a time of bitterness and discord, waning hopes and lower aims. The beauty, strength and grandeur of the ode reach far beyond any expression of strictly personal feelings. Moreover the symbol of the rock in a stormy sea is not a symbol of weakness or despair. The evils listed by the chorus exist, but from the beginning of the play Oedipus has shown that he can stand up to them. He does not feel, as in a similar situation Milton's Samson does,

> faintings, swoonings of despair
> And sense of Heav'n's desertion.

Nor could he say, as Samson says,

> Nor am I in the list of them that hope.

We do not know for what it is that he can hope and he himself only dimly knows it. Strangely, so far from feeling any 'sense of Heav'ns desertion', he feels just the opposite. His past life has been filled with suffering, but neither it nor the present moment is meaningless. Powerless for so long, he is now conscious of an inner power. Once more he is capable of doing good to his friends and harm to his enemies.

The last of these, his son Polynices, now comes before him and for his first two speeches Oedipus remains rocklike, silent and immovable. Polynices, though he has more spirit and more dignity than Creon, shows himself equally hypocritical and even more ambitious for himself. His pretended pity for his blind and outcast father deceives nobody, least of all Oedipus. He was one of those who mercilessly sent the old man into an exile of beggary, and, like the others, all he wants now is to make use of him. After Antigone has urged her father at least to listen to what the young man has to say, Polynices in his appeal to Oedipus speaks mostly about his own wrongs, which of course bear no comparison with those he has inflicted on his father, and of his pride in the great host of warriors which he has assembled against Thebes.

Oedipus' reply is a terrible one. Polynices will get no help from the father whom he has betrayed and persecuted. Nor will he ever storm the city of Thebes with his splendid host. On him and on his brother there rests a father's curse. Each will die at the other's hand.

Polynices is in despair. Without the help that he has asked for, he knows that his great hopes have gone. Antigone implores him to turn back before it is too late and not to bring ruin on his country, his army and himself; and in any case, she points out, his army will not follow him when they have heard of what has been foretold. But Polynices will go to meet his fate; he cannot bear to live in exile while his younger brother holds power in Thebes. As for the prophecy, he will say nothing about it; a good general publicises good news and conceals what is bad. So, with a courage born from a desperate pride, he rejects his sister's appeal. His last, somewhat pathetic, words are a prayer that, whatever may happen to him, at least his sisters, who are innocent in every way, may be spared all suffering.

And now the climax of the play and of Oedipus' life is at hand. Thunder, growing louder and louder, is heard and Oedipus, already a much greater and more potent figure than he was at the beginning of the play, seems to put on stature with every line he speaks. He knows that he is hearing the expected summons from the gods and sends urgently for Theseus. The chorus and the two girls are filled with awe and with terror. Oedipus is calm, confident and certain of himself and, when Theseus

A libation or offering to the gods, made by pouring a little wine on the ground

comes, he instructs him precisely what to do. To him alone will be revealed the place where Oedipus will leave this world and Theseus must reveal it to no one but his heir. So Athens will enjoy his protection for ever.

Now, instead of being led by others, Oedipus himself takes the lead. His sightless eyes can guide him and, telling Theseus and his daughters to follow in his footsteps, he goes forward alone.

The chorus have not long to wait before they hear all that can be told. One of Theseus' men returns and reports that Oedipus, stepping certainly as if the way were familiar to him, has led them into the grove and then stopped and instructed his daughters to bring water for washing and for making libations. He then said goodbye to them for ever and, as they wept at his words, there was silence, and then suddenly a loud cry 'Oedipus, Oedipus, why are we delaying on our way?' At this Oedipus had told the rest to leave the holy ground. Only Theseus was to remain. After that they had escorted the girls on their way and then looked back. All they could see was Theseus standing alone, shading his eyes with his hand as though from some strange and awful sight. Oedipus had vanished and no one except Theseus could tell how. There had been no violence of wind, thunder or lightning; it had been a gentle passing away either into the air or into some invisible fold in the ground, an end without sorrow or pain, wonderful beyond any.

The play ends with lyric passages of speech between Theseus, Antigone and the chorus. Theseus will enjoy the everlasting protection of the power which the dead Oedipus has now become and will respect his last wishes. Antigone will go back to Thebes to try, if she can, to make peace between her brothers. For the chorus 'nothing is here for tears'; these things have been in every way ordered as was right.

Sophocles' last play has often been compared with Milton's *Samson Agonistes*, the only good play in English which has been structurally modelled on Greek tragedy and which was written by one who was not only a great poet but who knew Greek as well as or better than any other English poet ever has known it. At the time when he wrote this play Milton, like Oedipus and like Samson, was himself blind; he had not, indeed, played such a distinguished part in political or military life as had those heroes, or, for that matter, as had Sophocles himself; but his part had been considerable, his hopes for the future almost unbounded; he had seen the failure of all his hopes and the collapse of the causes on which he had spent his eyesight and the best years of his life. He, like Samson and, in a somewhat different way, like Oedipus, had felt himself dedicated, chosen by God or the gods, for some great work and in his heart he could echo Samson's words:

> Promise was that I
> Should Israel from Philistian yoke deliver;
> Ask for this great Deliverer now, and find him
> Eyeless in Gaza at the Mill with slaves.

The pride and pathos of these words may remind one also of Oedipus, the man who by his native intelligence was able to save Thebes from the Sphinx, who governed admirably and whose fall was more horrible and complete even than Samson's. But here the resemblance ends. Milton's Samson cannot in any way call God's justice to account. The words just quoted are immediately followed by:

> Whom have I to complain of but myself?

And it is perfectly true that the cause of his fall was in his infatuation for Dalila, in becoming 'fondly overcome by female charm'. No doubt Milton himself, who had also married 'a daughter of the Philistines', could again identify himself with his hero. Oedipus, on the other hand, as we have seen, will on no account admit that he is responsible for his own misfortunes or has deserved from the gods any punishment at all.

Milton, it seems certain, would have agreed with the chorus in *Samson Agonistes* that

> Just are the ways of God,
> And justifiable to Men.

Sophocles might have assented, with some reservations, to the first of these propositions; he would not have assented to the second.

To Milton a belief in both of them was vitally necessary for the maintenance and confirmation of his faith. It is very doubtful whether Sophocles would have regarded such precise definitions as particularly valuable and he certainly would not have thought them essential to the preservation of his morality, his patriotism or his religion.

In this distinction, if it is a valid one, Milton's puritanism certainly plays a large part. His insistence on the direct and personal relationship between the individual soul and God is of a kind that does not appear at all in fifth-century literature. And Milton's particular kind of puritanism, together with his own character, leads him sometimes into a kind of egotism which may make one think that, in his view, the relationship between himself or, for that matter, Samson, and God was of that special kind that is said to prevail between England and America.

The strength, and also the self-righteousness, of those who believe in this metaphysical special relationship between God and the individual are evident enough, and it is perhaps inaccurate to single out the Puritans as the chief, or only, believers in it. The idea in its full force may have come from the Hebrews and it was developed by such pre-Miltonic puritans as St Augustine, who were also influenced by the late Platonists. As a guide to action, a strengthener of one's opinions and a consolation in adversity this faith may be expressed, in very crude, but very widely believed, terms as follows: God is and must be absolutely just in His dealings with me: if I do His will, I must be acting rightly and I am confident that I do know His will: if things turn out unexpectedly and I am led into suffering or disgrace, it must follow that I have been guilty and I must bear my punishment, knowing that I have deserved it and that it is for my good.

Head of Hera, probably by Polycleitos, a younger contemporary of Phidias

Obviously such a faith can, as is evident in Milton's Samson, lead both to a sense of pride and grandeur and to the deepest humility. But to a Greek of the fifth or fourth century the pride would seem to be, to use an old-fashioned word, overweening and the humility would seem abject. Neither would appear to be based on sufficient grounds. It might be allowed that, if we could understand everything, the dealings of the gods with men might be found to be entirely just; but it would be regarded as the height of arrogance for any man to pretend that he understood the ways of the gods so well that he could make anything but the most tentative judgments on the subject. One might readily admit that many misfortunes seem inexplicable and may be said to 'come from heaven', but that does not mean that they are deserved. Many good men have obviously suffered through no fault of their own, and they would be lesser men, indeed positively servile, if they persuaded themselves that these sufferings were not only deserved but to be welcomed.

But Jewish, Christian and Puritan views have so permeated later centuries as to affect not only our way of thought but our language. The Greek word '*aitios*' can mean 'responsible for', 'guilty of', 'the cause of'; but two out of these three translations in English will convey a sense of sin or fault which may not be and often is not present in the Greek. We say quite naturally 'it was not my fault; it was your fault', and, however we use the phrase, we are indicating that someone has done something wrong and is, as we say, 'to blame'. Wrong-doing or moral fault may be, but need not be, implied by the Greek word or words which might be used in the same situation. Plutarch[1] tells us, for instance, that Pericles in his youth spent a whole day with the famous teacher and sophist Protagoras in discussing who or what 'in the strictest sense' could be held responsible for an event which had recently taken place. In an athletic contest a man had been accidentally hit and killed by a javelin thrown by one of the competitors. Who was, as we should say, 'responsible' or 'guilty'? Was it the javelin-thrower, the javelin, or the organisers of the contest? Such a discussion is unlikely to be held today, since, although we might attribute guilt or culpable negligence either to the athlete or to the officials, we could not find an inanimate object like a javelin 'guilty' or 'to blame' for anything. Nor, of course, could Pericles; he would merely be using a word, '*aitios*', which can imply both guilt and a merely neutral causality.

That Sophocles and the Greeks in general recognised perfectly clearly what guilt was is evident. Also to them guilt could involve actions which were not punishable by law. The sons of Oedipus and Creon have done nothing legally wrong, yet they deserve all the hatred and contempt which Oedipus pours upon them because of their unnatural feelings and lack of generosity. We happen to know that they will come to bad ends; but their actions up to now do not necessarily imply disaster; they may be 'hated by the gods', but so far the gods have done nothing about it. The only person in the play who has been visited by total disaster is Oedipus, who, in his own view and that of Theseus and finally even of the chorus, has done nothing to deserve it. He may indeed be held *aitios* for the death of his father and for his

[1] *Lives*, 'Pericles', XXXVI

mother's incestuous marriage, since he was the man who killed Laius and married Jocasta. But, as he insists over and over again, he cannot be considered either guilty or sinful.

What, one wonders, would Milton have made of the Oedipus story? In all probability he would not have touched it, since in his scheme of things a perfectly just God could not have allowed a perfectly just man either to do or to suffer what was done and suffered by Oedipus. There must have been some sin somewhere – which is indeed what the chorus think at first, until they change their minds under the influence of Oedipus' logic and Theseus' natural generosity and nobility. Samson will fit well enough into Milton's scheme. He ought to have been proof against the allurements of Dalila and can be held *aitios* in every sense for his blindness and his disgrace. That he is permitted before death to perform one last great act and to destroy his enemies is a mark of God's generosity to him, not anything that he deserves.

Oedipus, on the other hand, lacks even the consolation of reflecting that his sufferings are deserved; and, though at the end he certainly feels 'God not parted from him, as was feared', he says nothing to suggest that his final semi-deification or elevation to the status of hero either justifies or was meant to justify what has happened to him in the past. By Milton's standards, by ordinary human standards and by the standards often employed by characters in Euripides he seems to have had every right to rail at heaven, or to deny that the gods exist or, if they do exist, that they pay any attention to human affairs; and his glorious end cannot affect the arguments that could lead to these conclusions. Whether or not 'all is best', no such conclusion is demonstrated. The *Oedipus at Colonus* ends certainly in calm of mind, a serenity even more complete and satisfying than anything we feel at the end of *Samson Agonistes*. But it can scarcely be said that all passion is spent. The passion that was Oedipus remains, stored, as it were, in the earth and in the air, still powerful to help his friends and to hurt his enemies. It is not a solution which justifies the ways of God to men, though it does suggest that in some inscrutable way the great man is, whatever he does or suffers, dear to the gods. Human greatness exists and the gods exist. What relationship there may be between the two can, at best, be only dimly surmised.

Milton and, in his own way, Euripides are concerned with what God or the gods ought to be, and Milton, unlike Euripides, is convinced that he knows and that he can prove that what, to his mind, God ought to be, He is. Sophocles seems to be intellectually and theologically rather more modest than Euripides and a great deal more so than Milton. Yet in presenting to us man as he ought to be and the gods as they are, his art, in all its pity and its terror, can give us a comfort which we do not find in the confident assertion of a Milton or in the agonised questionings of a Euripides.

EURIPIDES AND INSECURITY

The Greek poet, George Seferis, who died in 1971, has written the following poem under the title of 'Euripides the Athenian'.

> He lived and grew old between the burning of Troy
> And the hard labour in Sicilian quarries.
>
> He was fond of rocky caves along the beach;
> Liked pictures of the sea:
> The veins of man he saw as it were a net
> Made by the gods for trapping us like beasts.
> This net he tried to pierce.
> He was difficult in every way. His friends were few.
> The time arrived and he was torn to pieces by dogs.

Seferis has here written not a piece of history or of literary criticism, but a poem; but in the course of doing so he has said much that may be valuable to a student of Euripides himself. Had Seferis been writing as an historian one would have read 'Athens' and not 'Troy' in the first line. Euripides was born in 480 just before the battle of Salamis. And if he remembered anything of the time he may have remembered the buring of Athens by the Persians and the crowds of refugees who fled across the straits to the island of Salamis where his father had an estate. Whether the great naval victory, which saved Athens and Greece, meant anything at the time to the child, we cannot know; but it cannot have meant so much as it did to Aeschylus, who had fought in it, as also at Marathon, or to Sophocles, who in the flower of his early youth is said to have led a choir in thanksgiving ceremonies to the gods who had preserved the city. However, like Sophocles, Euripides grew up in the years of Athenian glory. He was fifty at the time of the building of the Parthenon and in several of his plays from this period shows the same delight and faith in Athens and what she stood for that Sophocles shows to the end. His Theseus in the *Heracles* like the Theseus of the *Oedipus at Colonus*, is noble, just and merciful, one who represents

Medea murdering her child

Medea wished to injure the family of Peleas. First she impressed them by
cutting a ram to pieces and reviving it in their presence as a lamb. RIGHT:
Then when his daughters tried to rejuvenate their father in the same manner
she did not give them the right herbs so that he perished at their hands.

and recognises the will of his people and who holds that the duty and the pride of
Athens is to give help to the distressed. And there is no reason to suppose that
Euripides did not retain his patriotism and his concern for his city until the end of
his life. But it is exceedingly doubtful whether he retained the faith and the confidence
which he had when, in the first year of the great war with Sparta, he wrote the famous
chorus in the *Medea*; the same year, according to Thucydides, that Pericles delivered his
funeral speech. In this play, as in many others, Euripides investigates and challenges
conventional attitudes, but not yet that attitude of 'falling in love with' Athens and
of knowing that she deserves one's love. The dramatic occasion for this chorus is at
a point in the play when Medea, in Corinth, who has been wronged by her husband,
Jason, has told the women of the chorus of her resolve to murder her children. She
proposes also to murder Jason's new bride and her father, the King of Corinth, and
has just succeeded in extracting a promise from Aegeus, the King of Athens (who is
in complete ignorance of her designs), that he will grant her refuge in Athens, should
she ever be in need of it.

   The chorus of Corinthian women, while sympathising with Medea in so far as she

has been disgracefully treated by her husband, are, not unnaturally, shocked at the method she has chosen to take revenge. They beg her not to commit this terrible crime and ask her how she could, after having committed it, venture to enter a city like Athens, pure, holy and wise. The words which Euripides puts into their mouths are more abstract than those of Sophocles' old men of Colonus; they lack the intimate feel of the countryside and the active presence of divinity; but they are equally grand and moving and they show, or seem to show, a hope and a confidence that Euripides was seldom, or never, to reveal again. This is the Athens which Aeschylus, throughout his life, had reason to believe in and which Sophocles, against much evidence, believed in to the end. It is the Athens of a long tradition and yet of startling modernity, of wisdom, beauty, gaiety and love. But, even in a translation, the words can speak for themselves:

> From of old the children of Erechtheus are
> Splendid, the sons of blessed gods. They dwell
> In Athens' holy and unconquered land,
> Where famous Wisdom feeds them and they pass gaily

> Always through that most brilliant air where once they say
> That golden Harmony gave birth to the nine
> Pure Muses of Pieria,
>
> And beside the sweet flow of Cephisos' stream,
> Where Cypris sailed, they say, to draw the water,
> And mild soft breezes breathed along her path,
> And on her hair were flung the sweet-smelling garlands
> Of flowers of roses by the Loves, the companions
> of Wisdom, her escort, the helpers of men
> In every kind of excellence.

This ideal Athens, which to Aeschylus, to Pericles, to Phidias and to Sophocles seems to have been not only an ideal but an actuality, may, for all we know, have been an object which Euripides long contemplated; but its presence is less and less evident in his plays. The plots of these plays are, like those of the other tragedians, taken as a rule from the cycle of legends which dealt with those few generations of heroes the last of which was concerned in the burning of Troy. For the whole of this heroic age far the best known and most revered source was, of course, Homer himself; but for most of their plots the dramatists went outside the *Iliad* and the *Odyssey* and took their stories from the less perfect cyclical poetry dealing with either the homecomings from Troy or the past histories of the royal houses of Thebes or Argos or Corinth. These could not be considered, as Homer might be considered, as in any sense national epics; they were stories of the acts, sufferings and crimes of great men from a particular and ancient great period. The stories are often of savagery, treachery and brutality and the characters may be 'good' but are often unequivocally 'bad'. In this respect they differ entirely from the characters in Homer, whose world is, for all its suffering, violence, death and sorrow, purged of vice and of the baser passions. All the characters in the *Iliad*, with the single exception of the unheroic Thersites, are 'good'. Hector may acknowledge some shortcomings in his brother, Paris; but all the same Paris is a splendid figure. Helen may, at times, hold herself responsible for all the suffering which the war has brought to Greeks and Trojans alike; but those who suffer most, such as Priam and Hector, are invariably kind to her and it is generally felt that it is not her fault. It would be granted that to run away in battle or to be lacking in generosity are blameworthy actions; but when, for once, Hector runs away from Achilles or Achilles behaves with shocking brutality to Hector's dead body, these exceptional events are made understandable and arouse our sympathy rather than our disapproval. When looked at through the eyes of a citizen, whether in ancient Athens or today, Homer's world in which everyone is good and everyone may be unfortunate, where those difficult questions of personal or communal morality simple do not arise, may seem a quite impossible world. The miracle is that it remains perhaps the most perfect, satisfying and, in a sense, true world ever created or described by man.

But Homer's wide and precise vision is not suited to the art of tragedy which will depend on the consciousness of moral conflict and which will grow up in a period of keen political debate. Aeschylus must take a very different view of Helen from that of Homer. In the *Iliad* the old men of Troy, seeing Helen pass, think of her as 'strangely like one of the immortal goddesses' and, while they deplore the fact of the terrible war, are not surprised that Greeks and Trojans suffer so much and so long for her. But this tolerant attitude is impossible to Aeschylus. To him Helen is more like an avenging fiend than a goddess; she and Paris must bear their dreadful weight of responsibility for the long and unnecessary agony of the war. And, incidentally, he would have been, I fancy, profoundly shocked by the use made of Helen by the modern poet, Yeats. The line:

Was there another Troy for her to burn?

with its implied suggestion that there could be anything glorious in such a responsibility would no doubt have puzzled him since the romantic exaltation of destruction was a sentiment unknown to him as it was unknown to Homer. If, however, he had been able to make anything of the line at all, he would have regarded it as impious or positively wicked.

The epic material, then, which was found useful by the dramatists is not found at all in Homer, or is only on the periphery of his poem. The crime of Clytemnestra and Aegisthus is known to him and is treated as something horrible and unnatural, but it is not an integral part of the *Odyssey*. Indeed, odd as it may seem, Homer is the only one of the great writers in the world who almost perfectly fulfils the requirements of Mr Podsnap in never provoking blushes in the 'young person' of Mr Podsnap's imagination.

But the material favoured by the tragic poets is very blush-making indeed. Cases of incest, parricide, madness, rape, seduction abound. Yet in the work of Aeschylus and Sophocles these facts of life, unpalatable as they must be to Mr Podsnap, are invested with such grandeur and even nobility that only to a Podsnap could they be really shocking. Clytemnestra's crime is terrible indeed, but she is a grander figure even than Lady Macbeth and less repulsive than either Regan or Goneril. The Creon of the *Oedipus at Colonus* is a mean and blustering tyrant, but he is an exception. On the whole kings and queens, whatever their vices, retain their dignity even in the later work of Sophocles. The Odysseus of his *Philoctetes* is certainly an unscrupulous and modern politician, very unlike the hero of the *Odyssey*, but, if his chief aim is success, he can appreciate and even sympathise with the claims of honour and is far removed from the perfidious Ulysses of Virgil's *Aeneid*.

It may be said, then, that, in spite of the violence and horror of their themes and in spite of their practical knowledge of the miseries of war and of the duplicities of politics, the early dramatists retained in the tone and treatment of their material very much of the nobility of the Homeric vision. They ask or imply questions that never occurred to Homer, but they still accept much of his morality and of his sense of a vivid and a more or less intelligible world, where life, whatever its disappointments and in spite of its inevitable end, can be valuable and splendid and rich with meaning, if only for a few moments.

I do not know whether or not by his phrase 'the burning of Troy' Seferis intended to imply anything of this general, shared and, in a sense, traditional outlook into which Euripides was born. But his reference to 'the hard labour in Sicilian quarries' is clear enough. He is thinking of the passage in Thucydides[1] which describes the end of the great and fantastically ambitious Athenian expedition against Syracuse, which, in the hopes of its sponsors, was to be the prelude to the conquest of Sicily, Italy and Carthage. Owing to a combination of circumstances in which folly, misguided superstition, treachery and sheer bad luck all played a part, the expedition ended in complete disaster. Two fleets were wiped out and the army was destroyed. Many were massacred and the generals were put to death by the Syracusans. One of these was the virtuous and, up to that time, successful Nicias of whom Thucydides writes:

> ... he was killed, a man who, of all the Hellenes in my time, least deserved to come to so miserable an end, since the whole of his life had been devoted to the study and the practice of virtue.

The prisoners were herded together in the stone quarries. Thucydides describes their plight as follows:

> Those who were in the stone quarries were treated badly by the Syracusans at first. There were many of them, and they were crowded together in a narrow pit, where, since there was no roof over their heads, they suffered first from the heat of the sun and the closeness of the air; and then, in contrast, came on the cold autumnal nights, and the change in temperature brought disease among them. Lack of space made it necessary for them to do everything on the same spot; and besides there were the bodies all heaped together on top of one another of those who had died from their wounds or from the change of temperature or other such causes, so that the smell was insupportable. At the same time they suffered from hunger and from thirst. During eight months the daily allowance for each man was half a pint of water and a pint of corn. In fact they suffered everything which one could imagine might be suffered by men exposed in such a place. For about ten weeks they lived like this all together; then, with the exception of the Athenians and any Greeks from Italy or Sicily who had joined the expedition, the rest were sold as slaves.

The news of the disaster in Sicily reached Athens when both Sophocles and Euripides were old men, and Sophocles was one of the commissioners appointed to deal with the crisis. There is no reason to suppose that this disaster and the knowledge of the sufferings that it entailed led to any feeling of defeatism in the case of Euripides any more than it did in the case of Sophocles or of Thucydides or that he felt any more keenly than they did the horrors of the Sicilian quarries. And in fact, contrary to the expectation of most of Greece, the catastrophe in Sicily did not end the war.

[1]Thuc. VII, 86–7

Athens fought on for eight more years and, with that almost incredible resilience which she had shown before in her history, won victories which, had she been wise as well as valiant, would have enabled her to end the war on terms favourable to herself. Yet in the poem of Seferis the phrase 'hard labour in Sicilian quarries' does, in its emphatic position, seem to be particularly appropriate to Euripides. For, patriotic as he may have been, and probably was, in his private and his public life, one cannot help feeling that in his particular kind of patriotism Pericles would have found something lacking, as he would not have found in the patriotism of either Sophocles or Thucydides, both of whom felt the horrors of war as keenly as anyone could feel them.

These two, however, seem to have kept some or all of the confidence they had once had and which Euripides too seems to have had while Pericles was alive. Euripides, on the other hand, in his later work, brilliant, compassionate, moving and strangely modern as it is, reveals something very like a failure of nerve. To this aspect of his work we shall return later. 'The Sicilian quarries' and some other phrases in Seferis' poem are suggestive of it.

Among these phrases are the lines:

> The veins of man he saw as it were a net
> Made by the gods for trapping us like beasts.

For in Euripides the ways of the gods to men are, as a rule, unpredictable or malicious. His gods may justly inspire fear, but very seldom respect. The young man Ion, in the play of that name, has indeed a touching devotion to the god Apollo whom he serves, who is, in fact, his father; but Apollo remains emotionally remote. In only one of the nineteen extant plays, the *Hippolytus*, is there a relationship of confidence and trust between man and god; but the goddess Artemis, who loves Hippolytus and to whom the young man is devoted, proves wholly incapable of saving him from the cruel and vulgar spitefulness of her sister-goddess, Aphrodite. The pardonable errors or forgetfulness of men are, in Euripides, visited by the most frightful consequences. A trifling mistake in judgment and its results will remind us of Virgil's words:

> *ignoscenda quidem, scirent si ignoscere manes*

('forgivable certainly, if only these dreadful powers had any conception of foregiveness'); but the gods do not forgive and they are scarcely capable even of feeling. Artemis, the most kindly of all of them, can say a few consoling words to her favourite, Hippolytus, as he is dying in agony; she can inform him, as though that were any consolation, that in the course of time she will get even with Aphrodite by killing another innocent young man whom Aphrodite loves; but she cannot bear to stay with Hippolytus to the end.

> Farewell. For I am not allowed to see the dead,
> Or stain my eye with the last gasps of dying men;
> And you I see already near that evil thing.

Dionysian revels. God of Wine, Dionysus was more important as the personification and leader of a religion of emotion.

There is more worth and dignity in the words with which the dying Hippolytus answers her:

> O farewell, blessed maiden, go upon your way.
> Easily now you leave our long companionship.

And Artemis is the most human of all the gods in Euripides. She did not positively organise the agony and destruction of Hippolytus; she merely did nothing to prevent it.

There are other gods and goddesses in Euripides who show either no moral qualities at all or ones which we would regard as bad or shameful. The Apollo of the *Ion* behaves like a particularly mean type of seducer of young women; the Dionysus of the *Bacchae* is a horrifying example of sheer cruelty.

Dionysus brandishing a fawn, 480–470. According to myth, used in The Bacchae, *under his influence bands of women in a state of ecstasy tore animals or even a child to pieces and ate the bleeding stumps.*

Yet it would be utterly wrong to maintain that Euripides is writing like a modern rationalist and aims to discredit superstition and to advocate some more enlightened view of things. Extremely difficult as it is to reach a clear idea of precisely what Euripides, or any of his contemporaries, meant by 'the gods', of one thing we may be certain – that Euripides was what we should call a deeply religious man. What he lacks is faith, the kind of certainty in man or god or both which, under whatever difficulties, is to be found in both Aeschylus and Sophocles. And this combination of the desire for and the lack of faith marks the beginning of the end of Periclean Athens and will lead to new departures.

It is often dangerous to regard the words of a chorus as expressing the views of the dramatist, but one may reasonably guess that in one chorus, again from the *Hippolytus*,

Euripides is expressing, rather pathetically and rather naïvely, a personal dilemma. He writes:

> Greatly indeed it will ease me of grief, when it comes to my mind,
> The thought of the gods,
> Yet, though guessing in hope at their wisdom,
> I am downcast again when I look at the fortunes and actions of mortals,
> For they alter, now here and now there;
> Man's life has no fixed station
> But is mutable always.

There may well seem to be nothing very original here. The other two dramatists would certainly concur in this view of the mutability of human affairs and they too would be downcast, to use no stronger word, when they considered the changes and

Dionysus with his ass, c.450.

chances they could see all around them. But in Euripides one seems to detect a frantic longing for security, for an almost mathematical assurance, that might appear to Aeschylus or to Sophocles as, while understandable, somewhat hysterical. For Euripides feels, in a way which they do not feel, that somehow the gods *ought* to be making things work better, and this intense feeling can have the result of depriving men of their responsibility. The old attendant of Hippolytus early in the play begs the goddess Aphrodite not to take too seriously the young man's foolishness in giving to her less honour than he gives to Artemis. And, in a thoroughly Euripidean way, he adds:

> Gods should be wiser and more moderate than men.

The whole action of the play will show that they are not, that Aphrodite is a savage, all-powerful and entirely unmerciful force who will destroy not only Hippolytus because of a minor fault, but the innocent Phaedra and the devout Theseus.

There are times, certainly, when the gods and goddesses of Euripides can almost be described in terms of forces of nature or psychological drives rather than as personal deities. And there are a few examples of the psychological drive being, as it were, self-sufficient and not needing the intervention of any divine power. For instance it is not Aphrodite, the goddess of love, who dominates the action of the *Medea* and indeed by Medea herself the goddess is scarcely mentioned. To a large degree Medea is in control of the action herself; she knows what she wants and she gets it with all the determination of a Clytemnestra. Yet the revenge which she seeks involves the murder of her own children and this is an act from which she instinctively shrinks. She is forced into the act partly by the logic of her position and by her own strength of character; but her own account of it is that she is being impelled by her '*thumos*', a word which here means a passionate self-assertion springing from a consciousness of her own value and an injured pride. Achilles also reacted passionately when he felt himself wronged, but his reaction was within limits. Medea's *thumos* carries her into actions from which even Clytemnestra would turn away. It is her successful self-assertion, perhaps, which, somewhat strangely, has made her a heroine among some modern feminists, none of whom, we may be sure, would contemplate the murder of her children; and it is her lack of any conception of a limit which shocked Aristophanes and some of Euripides' contemporaries, though they may well have been shocked also by the fact that at the very end of the play Medea is allowed to escape from the consequences of her crime by the convenient appearance of a winged and magic chariot sent to her by her grandfather, the god Helios. Thus in this play the gods, if they do not instigate, at least condone crime.

Medea, then, (apart from her miraculous escape) is in many ways a modern figure. She would not be out of place in Ibsen. She is, as we say, in the grip of passion, but the passion is her own and is not forced on her from outside as it is in the case of Phaedra in the *Hippolytus*, who, with every intention of living a happy and virtuous life, finds herself carried away against her will by a guilty passion for her stepson. By her also Aristophanes was shocked and, though her case and that of Medea are very different, he may have been shocked for the same reason.

It is often said that what the critics of Euripides objected to was the realism which he allowed on the stage. There is some, but not, I think, very much justice in this view, and certainly in his comedies Aristophanes makes considerable play with Euripides presentation of kings dressed as beggars (like Menelaus in the *Helen*), heroes who speak like contemporary sophists (as they often do) and all the rest. But no one can possibly maintain that realism was a new thing on the tragic stage. There is nothing in Euripides so realistic in the sense of being unpleasantly and (from the point of view of romantic heroism) squalidly actual as Sophocles' Philoctetes, who is shown on the stage not only in rags but in such stinking rags that no one can come near him and who, when in the pangs of his disease, breaks out into roars of agony and complaint. Indeed it would be possible to argue that Euripides, with his frequent use of the *deus ex machina* and other devices, was in the ordinary sense of the word less rather than more realistic than Sophocles. And Aristophanes parodies this lack of realism (the beautiful monodies in which there is more sound than sense, the miraculous rescues and escapes) as often as the more realistic aspects of his work.

And yet the realism of Euripides does exist. It has little or nothing to do with stagecraft or with plot. Nor does it imply or depend upon a rationalization of the divine, a substitution of elemental or psychological drives for the specific deities or for the more generalised 'the gods'. Euripides does at times come close to such a substitution and he is apt to make use of philosophical concepts of the time, such as Aether or Mind, where the other dramatists would be less explicit. He will argue about anything and his arguments reflect all the intellectual currents of his day. But he lacks altogether the rationalistic faith that everything is capable of an intelligible and satisfactory explanation, that, with appropriate psychological, educational and political adjustments, things will in the end work very well, that the gods either do not exist or can be wholly humanised. In spite of the modernity of his language he is less rational at heart than Pericles, Sophocles or Thucydides. Old Tiresias, in the *Bacchae* (Euripides' last play) will come out with a scientific explanation of the unlikely story that Dionysus was born after having been snatched from his mother's womb and sewn up in the thigh of Zeus and he will attempt to rationalise the gods as being simply names given to the necessary substances by which men live (Demeter = Bread and Dionysus = Wine); but the whole force of the play is thoroughly anti-rational. We find that Dionysus is something very different from a useful substance which can quench thirst and make men glad, and something very far even from a vague and kindly power making for men's good. Instead he is shown as a very real Being, unpredictable and beyond comprehension, without mercy and indeed enjoying the refinements of his own cruelty, one who demands not so much respect as abject obedience. No such monster as this is to be found among the gods and goddesses of Homer.

Again the question of how far Euripides believed in such maleficent powers as his Aphrodite or Dionysus is as insoluble as are the questions of the precise theological beliefs of Aeschylus or Sophocles. We may say, if we like, that Euripides is merely hypostatising those elements in the irrational psyche which he recognised in the observed behaviour of human beings. And we may say, though again it will not help us much, the same about some of the manifestations of the gods in Aeschylus and in Sophocles. None of the three dramatists would claim to understand the gods and all of them would agree that some of the actions which we attribute to them are beyond human understanding. It would not be fair to say that Aeschylus and Sophocles are conventional while Euripides is not; and it would not be fair to say that Euripides was more alive to the sufferings and agonies of mankind than were the other two dramatists. One might say with no hint of condemnation, that Euripides was less able than his predecessors to face these inevitable sufferings and agonies with fortitude. When Aristotle calls Euripides 'the most tragic' of the poets, part of his meaning may be that he is the one most lacking in hope.

His views of man and his views of the gods are, of course, interdependent. He had seen, as Sophocles and Thucydides had seen, the Athens which he had celebrated in the chorus of the *Medea* degenerate in the stresses of war, plague and party strife into something very unlike that ideal city of light; and perhaps he was less impressed than others by the amazing resilience and courage which in the darkest times the Athenians still showed and which, in spite of their folly and their mistakes, might still seem to justify the confidence which Pericles had had in his fellow citizens. He searches for explanations and sometimes seems to hurry almost feverishly among them, but his conclusions are lacking in force or assurance. Thucydides, who saw at least as keenly as Euripides the course of events and the deterioration of what to him too had been a splendid ideal, gives his own considered judgment in these words:[1]

> In times of peace and prosperity cities and individuals alike follow higher standards, because they are not forced into a situation where they have to do what they do not want to do. But war is a stern teacher; in depriving them of the power of easily satisfying their daily wants, it brings most people's minds down to the level of their actual circumstances.

Euripides, for all we know, might have considered this explanation a true one, as it obviously is. But it would not have satisfied him. To Thucydides war came as the result of a political decision which might be wise or unwise. All wars entail suffering and in all of them there must be an element of the unpredictable which may falsify calculation. In the case of the war with Sparta Pericles was, for instance, unable to have allowed for an utterly unexpected event like the plague, which had terrible effects in Athens; but his calculations and his estimate of probability had been so accurate that, in spite of the plague, which he could not have foreseen, Athens would have won the war easily if only her statesmen had avoided the mistakes against which Pericles had warned them. The war was justified by the fact that on its successful conclusion depended the existence of the Athenian way of life, which, in turn, depended on the retention of her empire. It was also justified by the fact that there was every evidence that it could be won; and, if further justification were required, it could be observed that Athens, by her very existence, gave to the rest of Greece and to the world something which no other power could give.

As for the evils and cruelties of war, they are very real to him, but they are, at least to some extent, understandable, or predictable, and a part of human nature, which does not alter greatly, being capable under appropriate conditions of rising to great heights or sinking to great depths. But this sensible and in a way clinical view of history does not in Thucydides and cannot in anyone else lead to despair. The possibility of good is as great as the possibility of evil and Thucydides believes that the results of his research will be 'judged useful' by subsequent generations who, he assumes, will aim at finding the good and avoiding the evil. As for the gods, they only enter his calculations in so far as men themselves may be affected by the beliefs they entertain of them.

[1]Thuc. III, 81.

Dionysus simply drunk

OVERLEAF: *Gravestone showing a Greek hero, Echelos, paying more attention to Basile, whom he is rescuing from the underworld, than to the horses, who are appropriately having to struggle uphill. Hermes, who shows the way, probably held a painted torch in his left hand.*

Euripides, of course, is writing poetry not history, though with him, as with the other poets, history permeates his thought. The gods are part of the conventional and chosen material of his poetry and, whatever his precise beliefs about them may have been, his treatment of them differs widely from the treatment given to them by either Aeschylus or Sophocles. In Aeschylus the gods are responsible for terrible things, but their action can always be, however indistinctly, justified. The crimes of the house of Atreus deserve punishment and the long chain of sin and counter-sin will lead in the end to the far-off divine event of the establishment of a better and more civilised system of justice. In Sophocles the wholly innocent, such as Antigone or Philoctetes or Oedipus, may be visited by the most dreadful sufferings, but they are never deprived of all responsibility and they always retain their essential greatness. The actions of the gods towards them may be difficult or impossible for us to understand; they are never represented as positively malignant or irresponsible. And, while no man can guard himself against all that may befall him, men still act in accordance with their own natures. They are never reduced to the status of helpless puppets.

But in Euripides this is not so. The gods are not represented as working towards any ultimate good, nor are they even allowed to be all-powerful yet incomprehensible; they are often either wholly indifferent or positively evil. They torture men for the spiteful gratification of their own vanity or pique, and part of the torture is that they do not allow men to retain their true characters or to recognise their own identities. If, outside the late romantic comedies, there are any 'good' characters in Euripides, they are usually to be found in the persons of slaves or people of humble station, such as the good peasant whom Electra has been forced to marry. These individuals are fortunate in so far as their low station has concealed them entirely from the attention of the gods. Even in the late romantic comedy of the *Helen*, where the theme is the simple one of escape, love rewarded and life happy ever after, an important part of the theme is in the demonstration that the whole heroic world of the Trojan War was a colossal fraud and delusion, that Helen herself had never been to Troy, and that Greeks and Trojans alike were pointlessly slaughtered year after year to gratify the spite of goddesses who had done less well than they thought they should have done in a beauty contest.

It is in this sense that we may say that Euripides saw the veins of man

> as it were a net
> Made by the gods for trapping us like beasts.

He indeed 'tried to pierce' this net, but, to judge from his later plays, his efforts were not successful. The Aphrodite of the *Hippolytus* has all the vices of a vain and spiteful woman and combines this with an irresistible power. But the Dionysus of Euripides' last play, the *Bacchae*, lacks even what respectability there may be in a bad example of human nature. He is inhuman and diabolical, a shapeless and irresponsible malevolence.

Dionysian revel turning to chaos

OVERLEAF: *Dionysus with actors, who hold masks, c.400. Drama has its origin in his cult.*

ΙΑ   ΔΙΟΝΥΣΟΣ

The *Bacchae* is the last of the great tragedies of the Athenian stage. It is a masterpiece and, in spite of the disruptive forces in it which we have noticed, it retains the form and something of the manner of the fifth-century tragic style. For many years the tragedies of Aeschylus, Sophocles and Euripides continued to be shown; but no other tragedian of comparable stature was to appear until the time of Shakespeare.

As for Euripides himself, it would be wrong to take at their face value the words of Seferis, 'his friends were few'. In fact we know very little about his life, and the tradition which, for his own purpose, Seferis makes use of in his poem depends on mere gossip or very unreliable evidence. We know for a fact that he once went to Sicily on an official embassy, and in all probability he fulfilled the ordinary obligations of a citizen, serving in the army from time to time. Had he evaded military service it is almost certain that Aristophanes would have had something to say about it. He was evidently interested in the philosophical speculations of the time and may well have studied under Anaxagoras and known the leading scholars of the day. His tragedies are said to have been greatly admired by Socrates and we may guess that what particularly pleased the philosopher was Euripides' dialectical skill and psychological insight – although it must be owned that guesses about Socrates are not easy to make confidently.

Dionysian drinking jar

Dionysus singing, supported by Ariadne and escorted by Eros

Other pieces of tradition used by Seferis are that Euripides was in the habit of working by the sea in a cave on the island of Salamis, where his father had an estate. He is also said to have been one of the first to compile a library. He wrote the elegy for the Athenian soldiers who fell in Syracuse, a fact which conflicts with the view that he left Athens at the end of his life because of the hostility of his fellow citizens. Probably he accepted the invitation of King Archelaus of Macedonia, at whose court he died, in much the same spirit as the honoured poet Aeschylus accepted in his old age an invitation to Sicily. And the story that the death of Euripides was caused by his being torn to pieces by the king's hunting dogs is even more unlikely than the story that Aeschylus met his death as a result of an eagle dropping a tortoise on him in the mistaken belief that the bald head of the poet was a rock suitable for cracking shells. In the case of Euripides the story may have originated from the scene in the *Bacchae* where Pentheus is torn to pieces by the women, including his mother and her sisters, who are under the savage and delusive impulse of Dionysus.

Whether Euripides' personal friends were few or many, there is no doubt of the extent of his reputation. The fact that he won few first prizes in the dramatic competitions may indicate a conservative taste in the judges, but cannot be held as evidence of the poet's unpopularity with the audience. And the fact that he is constantly parodied and made fun of by Aristophanes merely shows that he was well known. Indeed Aristophanes' constant quotations and parodies of Euripides not only show that Aristophanes himself must have known almost by heart the work of the poet whom he is attacking, but that most of his audience must have known it equally well.

At any rate towards the end of his life Euripides seems to have become increasingly fashionable, not only in Athens but in the outposts of the Greek world. Plutarch[1] relates that many of those who managed to get home safely from the Sicilian disaster owed their safety to the fact that they had been able to remember choruses and fragments from his plays. Because of this some had been freed from slavery and others, lost and wandering after the final battle, had been given food and shelter.

Certainly after the close of the century Euripides seems to have become the most popular of the three tragedians. After the conquests of Alexander his work became known throughout Asia to the borders of India; and it remained popular long after the collapse of the empire of Alexander and of his successors. A gruesome example of this is to be found in Plutarch's[2] account of how the news of the defeat and death of the Roman general Crassus, the friend and ally of Julius Caesar, reached the court of the king of Parthia. This king was, says Plutarch, well acquainted with the Greek language and literature and on this occasion a Greek company was giving a performance of Euripides' *Bacchae* at the court. They had reached the part near the end of the play where Agave, the mother of Pentheus, enters triumphantly carrying the head of her son whom she and the other women have torn to pieces, believing that what they have destroyed is a lion. At this point the severed head of the old general and millionaire Crassus was brought in and was snatched up by the actor taking the part of Agave as he declaimed the lyrics which Agave addresses to the chorus. Every-

[1]*Lives*, 'Nicias', 29   [2]*Lives*, 'Crassus', 33

A Dionysian procession

one, it seems, was delighted at this importation of real life into the theatre.

An even longer future was to lie before those late so-called tragedies of Euripides which were in fact romantic comedies, the first kind of escape literature which had appeared on the Athenian tragic stage. With the end of the century the Old Comedy, the last master of which was Aristophanes, ended rapidly and completely. The New Comedy was to become in the hands of Menander a drama of romance and deception, types, manners and happy endings. The poetry and the theological gropings of Euripides had gone, but the wit, cleverness and realism remained. There are no more kings and queens, no more gods and heroes, no more tragedy. The drama is of common life, of money and private interests, of the quarrels and the reconciliations of lovers. Politics have ceased to be important; grandeur has given place to charm and wit, an idyllic or ironic sentimentality, the private interests of the ordinary man who is gradually ceasing to be a citizen of any particular city.

Strangely it is Euripides who, drawing his strength from the world of Pericles, ushers in the new and different age which is still part of our environment, though it is extremely doubtful whether he had any idea of the direction in which things were going. His position in the history of the fifth century is well summed up by C. M. Bowra[1] in the following words: 'For a period the new intellectual movements had given strength to the old outlook, then come into conflict with it, and finally done much to destroy it. Euripides illustrated these stages, and in so doing speaks for his age.'

[1]*Periclean Athens*, C. M. Bowra, Chapter VII, 'Poetry and Politics'. London, Weidenfeld and Nicolson, New York, The Dial Press, 1971

The precise and delicate temple to Athena Nike on the Acropolis, finished c.425

THUCYDIDES

LAW AND NATURE

Among the many antitheses and oppositions to be found in the thought and literature of fifth-century Athens and, it may be added, of subsequent ages including our own, is that between what is conventional, customary or legal and that which is thought of as natural. '*Nomos*' is a word which embraces a number of different, though related, meanings ranging from the normal way of behaviour, the traditional way of life, to a system of laws which may be either enforced from above or voluntarily accepted. '*Physis*' means 'nature' in the sense in which we say 'it is the nature of ice to be cold', but it also, and more importantly, implies the principle of 'natural' coming into being and growth. The two terms need not be, but also may be, mutually exclusive. We may believe, for instance, in 'natural law' or that it is 'the nature of man' to live in accordance with law or custom; but we may also believe that all laws and conventions are oppressive impediments to the free development of the 'natural' man. And there are, of course, any number of intermediate positions which can be taken up between these two extremes. It has indeed been found possible to go in either direction even further than these apparent extremes. We may believe that human nature is in itself so utterly debased and brutal that it is incapable of anything valuable except under the dictatorship of some higher power. Or we may believe that man 'in his true nature' cannot be anything but good. The first of these propositions is not easy to maintain, since, if man is so utterly debased 'by nature', no man could attain sufficient wisdom to exercise authority and, assuming that the authority were to be supernatural, no man would be capable of recognising it as such. And the second of these extreme propositions would be regarded, at any rate by a Greek of this period, as too much at variance with experience to be worth consideration, at least so far as political life was concerned; and it was in political life that he was interested. Socrates indeed claimed to hold such startling beliefs as that no one willingly acted wrongly and that it was better to suffer injustice than to act unjustly, but these paradoxes were found very irritating by all who were not Socrates' intimate friends.

Considerations of the good man, the good life, the just society and justice in the abstract were to play a great part in the philosophical thought of the next century,

The theatre of Dionysus with the best seats at the front shaped in marble, and marked with the names of those for whom they were reserved.

largely under the impulse of Socrates. All these subjects were, of course, also debated in the age of Pericles, but the tone of the discussion was different. The thought of Plato and Aristotle is abstract and speculative. Though both of them were ready to plan ideal constitutions, though Plato actually attempted to introduce one in Syracuse and though Aristotle supervised the education of Alexander the Great, neither of the two was active or effective in politics and both seem to have thought that, even if active intervention in the affairs of one's city might be the duty of a philosopher, it was none the less a very unpleasant duty indeed. It is an attitude very different from that commended by Pericles, for whom, as for most of his contemporaries, thought and action were never far apart.

A bald and bearded intellectual, perhaps Herodotus, copied from a work of the classical period

Thucydides, the greatest political theorist of his and perhaps of any time, is, in the aims he sets before himself, closer to Pericles than to the philosophers. He pays the strictest attention to facts and prides himself on the care which he has taken to establish them and on the accuracy of his reporting. But the whole of his activity is carefully and deliberately designed to be an aid to right action. Here he differs profoundly from his predecessor, Herodotus, who lived for some time in Athens, was a friend of Pericles and Sophocles and was awarded by the Athenians the most lavish literary prize for his *History* that had ever been given. Herodotus too wanted to get his facts right and was a most diligent enquirer. It is part of his charm that he reports so many of these facts. His *History* also has an aim. It is designed to lead up to the war between Greece and the Persians and this event is seen as the culminating episode in the long struggle between East and West, which goes back at least as far as the Trojan War. His theme is, as he says, 'the great and wonderful deeds, some done by the Greeks and some by the barbarians'. In a sense this is the old epic theme, the famous deeds of men. But the great heroic theme is not treated either in a Homeric or in an Athenian way. The great and wonderful deeds are splendidly narrated and, if the narrative lacks the deep seriousness that is to be found in different ways in both Homer and Thucydides, it has much more wit and charm than either of these authors had or cared to employ. The spirit behind Herodotus' *History* is the delightful and insatiable curiosity of an Ionian. This curiosity does not require a particular aim either in abstract truth or in political utility. It is enjoyed for its own sake and, if the information it gathers is, as is necessary, sifted and organised to some extent, nothing of interest or amusement is left out. 'History' in Herodotus retains its Ionian meaning of 'enquiry' and it is enquiry simply for the pleasure of knowing. The great and wonderful deeds culminating in the war with Persia are certainly eminently worth reporting, but so are the strange customs of remote Indian tribes, the animals and fabulous birds of Egypt, the architecture and religion of Babylon, the road system of Asia, mathematical and religious discoveries of the Egyptians, amours of kings and tyrants, origins of political systems and indeed anything else which happens to meet the eye and engage the attention of this magnificently and voraciously curious traveller.

Thucydides is at least as interested in facts as his predecessor was, but he does not bother to set down 'facts' which seem to him either improbable or irrelevant. His enquiry has a definite and practical aim; it is to understand the processes of history so that understanding may lead, if possible, to right and desirable action. He also is profoundly affected by the great and wonderful deeds of men, but he is much less willing to see greatness and wonder everywhere than is Herodotus. In fact he finds very little of either of them far outside his own times and his own country. In the first few sentences[1] of his *History of the Peloponnesian War* he writes:

> For though I have found it impossible, because of its remoteness in time, to acquire a really precise knowledge of the distant past or even of the history preceding our own period, yet, after looking back into it as far as I can, all the evidence leads me to conclude that these periods were not great periods either in warfare or in anything else.

So much for the Trojan War and indeed for any war fought before the fifth century. He admits that the Persian War was the greatest fought in the past, but even here 'the decision was reached quickly as a result of two naval battles and two battles on land.'[2] The sufferings and calamities which it caused and the magnitude of its effects were, he believed, inconsiderable when compared with those that occurred as a result of the twenty-seven-year war between Athens and Sparta.

He may well have been thinking of Herodotus when, early in his History, he insists again on the practical value of his work and, while disclaiming the merits of an entertainer, demands consideration on much higher and more extensive grounds. His words are:[3]

> And it may well be that my history will seem less easy to read because of the absence in it of a romantic element. It will be enough for me, however, if these words of mine are judged useful by those who want to understand clearly the events which happened in the past and which (human nature being what it is) will, at some time or other and in much the same ways, be repeated in the future. My work is not a piece of writing designed to meet the taste of an immediate public, but was done to last for ever.

[1]Thuc. I, 1   [2]Thuc. I, 23   [3]Thuc. I, 22

Among those elements of a romantic or mythological nature which he excludes from his work is any intervention in history by the gods. Herodotus, while carefully examining the motives and decisions of men, very often attributes the outcome or the origin of their action to 'a god', 'the gods' or 'the divine power'. This is never the case with Thucydides. For him the determining and operative causes of events are to be found in two categories and in two categories alone. One of these we would call economic or logistic, including natural resources, man-power, accumulation of capital, naval design and expertise, military tactics, features of climate and geography. The other is simply human nature, the *physis* of man, in its broad lines unchangeable, but capable of some variations and modifications depending on either economic or social factors. Basically, for instance, the savage and the civilised man may have the same nature, but there is a difference between the two, just as there is a difference between an Athenian and a Spartan, each of whom lives under different economic influences and social pressures or ideals. One of the grim conclusions which we can draw from Thucydides' analysis and which, no doubt, he would think it wise for us to 'judge useful', is that under the stress of war, revolution or other calamity these distinctions are likely to disappear. Athenian and Spartan will behave in much the same way and it is the way of a savage. This conclusion, expressed, as it often is, with terrifying force, cannot, of course, be thought of as either cynical or despairing. The values of civilisation are not debased by a recognition of how fragile is the structure on which they stand.

Many commentators have rightly pointed out the similarity between the method of Thucydides and that of the Hippocratic school of medicine which was flourishing at his time. These physicians also were eminently practical. They aimed at diagnosis through the thorough study of the symptoms and their basic assumption was the scientific one that all diseases spring from natural causes – changes in temperature, excesses or lacks of normal dietary requirements etc. Divine intervention, whether or not it might occur, was none of their business. The author of the treatise *On the Sacred Disease* takes exception to this particular disease, epilepsy, being singled out from all the rest. All diseases, he says, have physical causes and none of them is in a special class by itself. You can call them all human or all divine; it does not matter so long as you set about curing them on principles that have been discovered by human thought and experience.

Thucydides undoubtedly followed the same method and may well have been influenced by its medical practitioners. His account of the plague which hit Athens soon after the outbreak of war is a model of detailed analysis. He deals with the possible origins of the disease, the climatic conditions prevailing at the time, the behaviour of birds and animals, the symptoms of the disease at each of its stages, the effects of over-crowding the population inside the fortifications, and seems to leave nothing unsaid which a doctor would like to know. And, as he points out, since he caught the disease himself and was one of the few who recovered from it, he was in an excellent position to give an accurate report.

His scope, however, is wider even than that of medicine. The health or disease of

Map of alliances for the Peloponnesian War, 431–404

the body politic may be affected not only by external natural forces but also by man's own nature with its passions and aspirations which may be regulated or unrestrained by law and custom, which can be conscious or unconscious and which may themselves be a determining factor in the course of events. Thus Thucydides' account of the plague has much more than a medical importance and emphasis. His most impassioned sentences describe the effects of this catastrophe not on the bodies but on the minds of men and on the security of their institutions. He relates how,[1] when people realised that there was no remedy for a disease which struck equally at the rich and the poor, the good and the bad, they·began to stray in the direction of 'a state of unprecedented lawlessness', thinking only of the pleasure of the moment and indifferent to the claims, hitherto recognised, of morality and religion.

As for what is called honour, no one showed himself willing to abide by its laws, so doubtful was it whether one would survive to enjoy the name for it. It was generally agreed that what was both honourable and valuable was the pleasure of the moment and everything that might conceivably contribute to that pleasure. No fear of god or law of man had a restraining influence. As for the gods, it seemed to be the same thing

[1]Thuc. II, 51ff

The Pnyx, where Athenian citizens held meetings

whether one worshipped them or not, when one saw the good and the bad dying indiscriminately. As for offences against human law, no one expected to live long enough to be brought to trial and punished.

Such passages as this and the even more terrifying later chapters[1] which describe the effects of revolution in Corcyra and throughout the Greek world reveal much more than the accuracy and austerity of an analyst, more even than the pity of a sensitive man for human suffering and his indignation at the degradation of an ideal. They show a deep and strong moral sense which is as important a part of this historian's make-up and impulse as are his ability for close and reasoned analysis and his zeal for a truth that can be found useful. When he writes of 'what is called honour', it is certain that to him personally this was much more than a name. So in the chapters on the effects of revolution in Corcyra which entailed 'a general deterioration of character throughout the Greek world', the first sign of this deterioration which he mentions is this:

> The simple way of looking at things, which is so much the mark of a noble nature, was regarded as a ridiculous quality and soon ceased to exist.

[1]Thuc. III, 81–2

And there is no doubt of where his own feelings lie when he describes how, in these revolutionary situations, words began to take on new meanings:

> To fit in with the change of events, words, too, had to change their usual meanings. What used to be described as a thoughtless act of aggression was now regarded as the courage which was to be expected in a party member, to think of the future and wait was merely another way of saying that one was a coward; any idea of moderation was just an attempt to disguise one's unmanly character; ability to understand a question from all sides meant that one was totally unfitted for action. Fanatical enthusiasm was the mark of a real man.

No doubt when he was writing these words Thucydides was thinking not only of Corcyra but of Athens and of those politicians who came after Pericles, who distorted his policies and his ideals and who were, in Thucydides' view, wholly lacking in the signs of 'a noble nature'. Thucydides himself was, almost certainly, related to the great aristocratic leader Cimon and to Thucydides, the son of Melesias and bitter political opponent, as indeed Cimon had been, of Pericles. We do not know how it was that the historian, in his youth, forsook the traditions of his family and became an ardent supporter of the new Periclean system of total democracy and of antagonism to Sparta. However that may have been, it is certain that Pericles, the extreme democrat, had one point in common, apart from the fact that he too came from a noble family, with his conservative and aristocratic political opponents. He also had 'a noble nature' and, however advanced his thought or far-reaching his aims, he retained 'the simple way of looking at things' in which there was no trace of vulgarity, self-interest, cruelty, duplicity or ostentation. These ignoble qualities were certainly found by Thucydides in Cleon and in the statesmen after Pericles and they are important among the factors to which he attributes the failure of Athens to win the war and the general deterioration of character throughout the Greek world. We may say therefore that to Thucydides the presence or absence of these qualities can do something, even much, to determine the course of events. History may be conditioned but is not pre-determined by economic or logistic facts. Human nature may show all the variations between perfect health and incurable and incapacitating disease; but, within certain limits, men can choose health or sickness. Societies are likely, perhaps almost certain, to fall sick under the prolonged stresses of war, that 'stern teacher', or revolution or unexpected calamity. But they can be saved, preserved and bettered by a proper use of intelligence which, to be properly used, must be directed by a moral sense, 'the simple way of looking at things, which is so much the mark of a noble nature'.

This kind of moral sense is, I believe, a much more important element in Thucydides than is usually recognised. It is not a Christian morality, since it does not suggest that we should love all men or that God is Love. It is not Jewish, in the sense that it does not depend on instant and complete obedience to a divine authority. But it is thoroughly Greek. Some elements go back to Homer – the love of honour, the wish to excel, but only to excel within the conditions of honour, generosity and courtesy, the refusal, in Pericles' words, 'to fall below a certain standard'. Some are modern and of the fifth century – solidarity with one's fellow-citizens, justice, pity for the oppressed. These same qualities are to be found in the Oedipus and in the Theseus of Sophocles, and Thucydides, like Sophocles, holds out no assurance or certain hope that these qualities, admired as they are, will necessarily lead to success or will be rewarded by anything but the fame which is their due. In the plays of Sophocles, as is befitting on occasions which were religious as well as dramatic, the gods are often mentioned and sometimes intervene, though on the whole the actions of men move along their own paths and can be explained largely in human terms. But, whether or not Sophocles was a believer and Thucydides an unbeliever, each admires and affirms the same type of character and action. They would probably agree that this is what men ought to be, whether the gods are believed in or not.

There are some critics who maintain that Thucydides goes a long way further than this, that his *History* is written in accordance with the conventional model for tragedy, showing that *hubris* (in this case the *hubris* of Athens) is followed inevitably by *atê*, which must lead to disaster; and that *hubris*, the first step, involves an offence against the eternal laws of the universe, which may be called the laws of the gods. But, as we have seen, this theoretical model, useful to critics, is not always followed by the tragedians themselves and, when it is, is capable of various interpretations, not all of which are in any sense religious. And the evidence adduced to show that Thucydides, in the writing of his *History*, is guided or even influenced by religious or metaphysical consideration is, to me, entirely unconvincing.

No such considerations are involved in reaching the conclusion that over-confidence is likely to lead to serious, and possibly disastrous, mistakes in judgment; nor does the admission that the unpredictable can play an important part in events imply that in the unpredictable we see the hand of a god; nor does the recognition that a misguided and reckless policy will lead to situations of greater and greater danger indicate the inevitability of a judgment or retribution. Sometimes it does not occur.

Thucydides does indeed employ many dramatic expedients and among these is irony, the same kind of irony that we find often in Sophocles. It is this irony which is most often mistaken for something else by those who attempt to reveal what they consider to be the metaphysical and religious elements in the *History*. In this connexion the most quoted passage is the juxtaposition of the sentences ending Book V with those at the beginning of Book VI. The Fifth Book ends with the account of the Athenian subjugation of the small neutral island of Melos. In the most brutal and cynical expression of pure power politics that has ever been written, the Athenian envoys reject every claim of common decency, of justice and of religion that the Melians make. In the course of the debate the Melians admit that their strength is feeble compared with that of Athens, but at least their cause is just and it may well be, they contend, that the gods, knowing that they are standing for justice against injustice, will come to their aid and even out the odds. The reply of the Athenians is both devastating in its logic and shocking to anyone who, as Thucydides did, prizes 'the simple way of looking at things, which is so much the mark of a noble nature'. This, by the envoys, is now clearly regarded as 'a ridiculous quality'. They say[1]:

> So far as the favour of the gods is concerned, we think we have as much right to that
> as you have. Our aims and our actions are perfectly consistent with the beliefs men hold
> about the gods and with the principles that govern their own conduct. Our opinion of
> the gods and our knowledge of men lead us to conclude that it is a general and necessary
> law of nature to rule wherever one can. This is not a law that we made ourselves, nor
> were we the first to act on it when it was made. We found it already in existence, and we
> shall leave it to exist for ever among those who come after us. We are merely acting in
> accordance with it, and we know that you, or anybody else with the same power as ours,
> would be acting in precisely the same way.

Their case is based on knowledge of men, with which it is found that opinion about
the gods coincides. Later the Melians are warned not to be led astray by 'a false sense
of honour'. The Athenians admit that in some cases, where pride is affected, people
are restrained from doing the obvious and sensible thing by the thought that it is
dishonourable to give in gracefully to superior power. The result is that 'this thing
called dishonour, this word' leads them to surrender to an idea, while in fact they
plunge into a disaster 'in dishonour that is all the more dishonourable because it has
come to them from their own folly rather than their misfortune'.

Nevertheless the Melians decide upon resistance, putting their trust in the gods
and in help that may be sent by Sparta. The final comment of the Athenians is: 'You
seem to us quite unique in your ability to consider the future as something more
certain than what is before your eyes, and to see uncertainties as realities, simply
because you would like them to be so.'

Everything happens as the Athenians foretold. The Spartans send no help; the
gods do not intervene. After a brave resistance, the Melians are forced to surrender
and the Athenians put to death all the men of military age and sell the women and
children as slaves.

This concludes Book V. The next book begins with the words: 'In the same winter
the Athenians resolved to sail again against Sicily', and every reader would know
what that meant – the total destruction of the greatest expedition that had ever sailed
from Athens, a blow from which she would never recover. And when Thucydides
goes on to point out that the Athenians had very little idea of the size and strength
of Sicily or of how big a war they were taking on, one is naturally reminded of the
Melians who regarded the future as something more certain than what was before
their eyes, who could see uncertainties as realities and who found themselves in the
end utterly mistaken.

There are other ironic juxtapositions of the same kind in Thucydides; but this
one is perhaps the most striking. It does not, however, to my mind provide the
slightest evidence for supposing that Thucydides is asserting the existence of any
universal law, natural or divine, which guarantees the validity of morality or the
inevitable punishment of injustice. The Melians, who have done nothing wrong,

[1]Thuc. V, 108

come to the same bad end as the Athenians, who have. Moreover Thucydides was very far from thinking that the expedition to Sicily was bound to end as it did. He shows that with better management and even a little luck it would certainly have succeeded. He might well have admitted that both the attack on Melos and the expedition to Sicily sprung from qualities of recklessness and thoughtless aggression in the Athenian character which Pericles could hold in check, while his successors actually encouraged them. But this is a very different thing from suggesting that the military, though unjust, success of one operation determined or in any way influenced the military failure of the other. Indeed, if there is any such thing as divine justice, Thucydides gives us no reason for believing in it. If the gods felt any pity for the Melians, they did not show it any more than they did to the god-fearing and virtuous Nicias, who, in his last brave and desperate appeal to his broken army as it is trying to escape by land, attempts to comfort his men with the thought that, if any of the gods was angry with them at the beginning, they have already been sufficiently punished.[1]

> Other men before us have attacked their neighbours and, after doing what men will do, have suffered no more than what men can bear. So it is now reasonable for us to hope that the gods will be kinder to us, since by now we deserve their pity rather than their jealousy.

The hope may be reasonable, but it is as vain as was the hope of the Melians who had done nothing at all to incur divine displeasure. As for Nicias, who 'of all the Hellenes of my time least deserved to come to so miserable an end', he was put to death as a prisoner and for the survivors of his army there awaited the Sicilian quarries.

Thucydides, then, seems to see no law or force or principle in history which is not explicable in human or material terms. He acknowledges certainly that a part, and an important part, may be played by the unpredictable; but for him this is a word which means precisely what it says; no pattern can be discerned in the operations of chance, which is why he describes it as he does. Later theorists, in Hellenistic, medieval and modern times, have elevated Chance or Fortune or Destiny to the status of a divine power. Thucydides shows no tendency whatever to do this.

Thucydides' view of history, then, is in no way dependent on considerations of metaphysics or theology; but it would be very wrong to suppose that it is either materialistic or deterministic. True, 'human nature being what it is', similar courses of action in similar circumstances are likely, or even certain, at all times to lead to similar effects. But the courses of action themselves can be, and often are, the result of a free and deliberate choice between alternatives. If this were not so, men would be unable to learn from experience and no investigation of the past, however accurate and informed, could ever be 'judged useful'.

People are apt, certainly, both to attribute events to the wrong causes and also greatly to exaggerate causal elements which, though present, are not important. In

[1] Thuc. VII, 77

discussing the origin of the war, for instance, Thucydides states clearly the story of the disputes between Athens and the allies of Sparta which were connected with Corcyra and with Potidaea. These disputes were said to have caused the war and each side, of course, accused the other of having been first guilty of aggressive action. But to Thucydides[1] 'the real reason for the war is . . . most likely to be disguised' by a discussion of the rights and wrongs of these incidents. The real reason for it was the growth of Athenian power and the fear which this caused in Sparta. This is a conclusion which may seem to proceed from the same theory of history as that held by the Athenians at Melos, 'that it is a general and necessary law of nature to rule wherever one can'; and there are many passages in Thucydides which may be held to support the view that history is determined by a continual struggle for power and that political decisions are made solely for self-interest in the direction of the acquisition or retention of power. As we have seen, there are words of Pericles himself which may seem to fit in with this theory, but, as we have already hinted, it would be a mistake to understand them so.

The famous debate[2] on the fate of the population of Mytilene is an example of an argument which is conducted entirely in terms of political expediency, but which also contrives to indicate that it was not exactly in these terms that Thucydides himself saw the situation.

Early in the war, in the year after the death of Pericles, when Athens was still weakened by the plague, the Athenians were shocked to hear of the revolt of the

[1]Thuc. I, 23   [2]Thuc. III, 36–48

BELOW: *Part of a kleroterion, used to select jurors. Names of potential jurors were placed in the slots; a mixture of black and white balls were fed into a tube, (not shown) at random. Whether a candidate was selected for service or sent away depended on the colour of the ball which emerged when it was the turn of*

important city of Mytilene in Lesbos, one of the few of the original allies which still retained its own fleet and army and so had always held a privileged position in the Athenian League. The revolt had been organised, as always happened in such cases, by a pro-Spartan group in Mytilene and Sparta had sent out an expedition to help the rebels. This force was so incompetently handled by the Spartan admiral that it failed to achieve anything except to escape from an Athenian fleet. Meanwhile the Athenians had landed on the island; the democratic party in Mytilene, finding that their oligarchic opponents were less strong than they had thought, turned against them and forced them to surrender to the Athenians.

The event might be held to show that, even in difficult times, the Athenians could still rely upon the support of the majority of the people in an allied state. But this was not at all the way in which the Athenians looked at it. They had been extremely frightened not only by the ability of their enemies to gain power, if only temporarily, in an important allied city but by the fact that Sparta had actually dared to challenge them in their own seas, even though the challenge had been so feeble as to be almost ludicrous. And so they acted in one of those moods of anger, resentment and lack of thought which Pericles had been able to control or prevent, but which his successors rather tended to inflame. They passed a decree by which not only the prisoners, but the entire adult male population of Mytilene were to be put to death and the women and children sold as slaves.

Next day, however, according to Thucydides, 'there was a sudden change of feeling and people began to think how cruel and how unprecedented such a decision was'.

his row. OPPOSITE: *the tickets used in selection for civic duties.* BELOW LEFT: *juror's ballots, with solid hubs for acquittal and hollow hubs for condemnation.* BELOW RIGHT: *two waterpots, one emptying into the other. No speaker could continue for longer than this process took.*

In response to this change of feeling, the authorities agreed to reopen the question and a debate was held which is dramatically described by Thucydides. In his account the case for carrying out the decree is stated by Cleon, on whose motion it had been passed on the previous day; and the case for showing mercy is put by Diodotus, a character who does not appear elsewhere in the *History*.

With the precise arguments used on each side we are not now concerned; what does concern us is the fact that each side claims that its arguments are in no way influenced by considerations of compassion, decency or civilised behaviour. Cleon states bluntly that the empire is a dictatorship, that only fear can keep its subjects from revolt and that therefore terror should be employed in all such cases and especially in this one. He reinforces his argument with an appeal to what is, to him, righteous indignation. The Mytileneans, he says, have behaved so very badly that they deserve the harshest punishment that can be given them. The argument of Diodotus is much more subtle, but he is careful to point out that he too bases his case on the interest of the city and on nothing else.
And in his peroration he asks:

> If we are sensible people we shall see that the question is not so much whether they are guilty as whether we are making the right decision for ourselves. I might prove that they are the most guilty people in the world, but it does not follow that I shall propose the death penalty, unless that is in your interests: I might argue that they deserve to be forgiven, but should not recommend forgiveness unless that seemed to me the best thing for the state.
> Do not be swayed too much by pity or by ordinary decent feelings. I, no more than Cleon, wish you to be influenced by such emotions.

On the face of it, therefore, it might appear that this debate is an example of the same kind of cynical political realism as was shown later by the Athenian envoys in Melos. But to understand it in this way would be, I think, to mistake the intention of Thucydides. What Diodotus has done triumphantly and brilliantly is to meet Cleon on his own ground and to prove that *even here* Cleon's argument is not only brutal, but muddleheaded and politically dangerous. The fact that Diodotus deliberately excludes from his own argument considerations of pity and ordinary decent feelings does not indicate that either he or Thucydides regarded these considerations as unimportant; it merely shows that these feelings are not only natural but can be politically useful.

And in this debate Thucydides is interested, it seems, in demonstrating more than this. In introducing Cleon he writes:

> He was remarkable among the Athenians for the violence of his character, and at this time he exercised far the greatest influence over the Athenians.

The last statesman mentioned as having been far the most influential was Pericles, who, far from being remarkable for violence of character, is distinguished for just those qualities of nobility and of reasonableness which Cleon conspicuously lacks. And Cleon's speech is in some ways a frightening parody of Pericles. There are times when he employs phrases which are almost quotations from speeches which Pericles is reported as having made. But these near-quotations have the effect of so distorting the tone and the basic meaning of a Periclean pronouncement as to rob it of all profundity and distinction. Cleon is undoubtedly a clever demagogue and one can imagine that he was applauded by many of those who had in the past applauded Pericles and who may have believed that they were hearing the very arguments that Pericles had used, though in a form that was, by its very violence and brutality, easier to understand. Had not Pericles said that, whatever the rights or wrongs of holding power, Athens must keep her empire under control during the war? And when Cleon proclaimed that 'your empire is a dictatorship exercised over subjects who do not like it', was not that much the same thing, only perhaps expressed with a rather agreeable realism? And such people might be pleased rather than otherwise by those parts of Cleon's theory, if it deserves the name, which were in clear contrast with all the assumptions and beliefs on which Pericles' political views were based. While Pericles believes in generosity and in a self-sacrificing patriotism in pursuit of 'a great aim', Cleon regards generosity, like 'the simple way of looking at things' as 'a ridiculous quality', and his patriotism is naked and unashamed self-interest. Where Pericles is constantly emphasising the value of reasoned thought and discussion and regards these as especially the pride of the Athenian democracy, Cleon no doubt derived support from that section of the population which, even in Athens, was profoundly suspicious of the intellect and felt proud of their dubious talent for calling a spade a spade. Such people would be delighted by Cleon's contention 'that lack of learning combined with sound common sense is more helpful than the kind of cleverness that gets out of hand, and that as a general rule states are better governed by the man in the street than by intellectuals.'

Cleon, like Antony in *Julius Caesar*, seems to have represented himself, though violently and with a total lack of modesty, as a plain blunt man. He differs from Antony in that he really was one, so long as bluntness is not confused with honesty and plainness with an avoidance of sophistry. Diodotus or Thucydides, or both, show that this self-proclaimed realist is nothing of the kind, his argument self-contradictory and his supposed common sense a mixture of ignorance and bluster.

Diodotus' speech is subtle and devastating in its apparent politeness. Not that there is any doubt about his contempt for Cleon. He begins by saying:

I do not share the view which we have heard expressed, that it is a bad thing to have frequent discussions on matters of importance. Haste and anger are, to my mind, the two greatest obstacles to wise counsel — haste, that usually goes with folly, anger, that is the mark of primitive and narrow minds. And anyone who maintains that words cannot be a guide to actions must be either a fool or one with some personal interest at stake; he is a fool if he imagines that it is possible to deal with the uncertainties of the future by any other medium, and he is personally interested if his aim is to persuade you into some disgraceful action, and, knowing that he cannot make a good speech in a bad cause, he tries to frighten his opponents and his hearers by some good-sized pieces of misrepresentation.

The words may be those of Diodotus, or of Thucydides himself, but the voice is the voice of Pericles.

Cleon, as is soon shown, qualifies for both the categories of fool and knave; and his pretended realism is in fact an emotional reaction based on the anger that distinguishes 'primitive and narrow minds'. His flattery of the people and his declared admiration for the man in the street is preceded by the statement, impossible in the mouth of Pericles, that 'a democracy is incapable of governing others'. By incapacity he means a readiness to listen to discussion and to admit the possibility that one might have made a mistake.

Diodotus, by accepting for the purpose of his argument, Cleon's premises that mercy and decency should have no part in the decision and that the interests of Athens are alone important, is able to show that, even on these premises, Cleon's advice, if followed, would have the opposite result to that intended, that Athens would actually be harmed by the brutal sentence on the whole population of Mytilene.

It is a brilliant debating speech, very much in the manner of the time. Admirers of Euripides and indeed Euripides himself, if he had read it, would have thought highly of it. It does exactly what it sets out to do. It shows that, even on the lowest view of human nature, Cleon's brutality cannot be justified and it points out incidentally that Cleon's expression of this view is vitiated by a lack of logic and by the decisive influence of that very emotionalism (though in the form of savage anger rather than of pity or compassion) which he pretends to be avoiding.

That the existence and the importance of such feelings as pity and compassion are in fact recognised by Diodotus, by the Athenians and by Thucydides himself is indicated by various passages in Diodotus' speech and, even more clearly, by the narrative framework in which the speech is set. To begin with, it was the 'sudden change of feeling' in the Athenians that led to the reopening of the debate. People began to think what a cruel and monstrous thing it was which they had decided to do. And, in the end, when the motion of Diodotus has been carried, comes the account of the boat race between the two triremes, the first of which, with orders for the massacre, has twenty-four hours' start over the second one which brings notice of a reprieve. Those in the second trireme exerted themselves to the utmost and rowed day and night, but Thucydides is careful to point out that in arriving, as they did, just in the nick of time, they were helped by the fact that the crew of the first trireme 'was not hurrying on its distasteful mission'.

There follows another of those dramatic juxtapositions, one of which we have noticed already. Immediately after the account of the debate of Mytilene comes the account of what happened during the same summer in the small city of Plataea, an old ally of Athens, which had been for some time invested by the Spartans and the Thebans. After a very gallant resistance the garrison had been starved into surrender and appealed to the Spartans for mercy. Their crime had been to defend themselves against unprovoked aggression from Sparta's ally, Thebes; their record in the wars with Persia had been, though smaller in scope, as glorious as that of Athens and their security had been guaranteed for ever by a Spartan king. A committee of judges from

The small temple of Athena Nike had a narrow path between it and a considerable drop. This was dangerous for crowds and a balustrade was added on the outside of which were reliefs, including this one. Nike is loosening her sandle in order to bring the victory offering barefoot.

Sparta condemned them all to death; women and children were sold as slaves, and the city razed to the ground.

Apart from the emphasis which comes from juxtaposition in the narrative Thucydides makes no attempt to draw a parallel between the obviously cruel and unjust action of the Spartans and the equally cruel action almost, but in the end not taken by the Athenians in Mytilene. Nor does he indicate in the case of Sparta, as he did in the case of Athens, that pity and decent feeling were in fact on the side of national interest. By destroying Plataea Sparta strengthened her important alliance with Thebes and though her action provided further evidence, if this were needed, that her pretensions as a 'liberator' could not be taken very seriously, this did nothing to weaken her position in the war any more than Athens was weakened later on by her action against Melos.

We can find plenty of evidence to show that Thucydides himself valued the ordinary and old-fashioned behaviour which goes with a rational obedience to the laws and is influenced by feelings of mercy, kindness, generosity and a sense of honour; to him these qualities are far from being ridiculous. We may even be able to show that he believed that, at least in normal circumstances, this kind of honesty, apart from being good in itself, is actually the best policy. But there is no reason for supposing that he ever thought that this is always or necessarily the case. Outrageous behaviour, offences against the laws of gods and men, may, through the resentment provoked, be a factor in bringing about what may be called retribution. But this will not happen unless the righteous resentment is adequately armed. History does not indicate that virtue is necessarily and invariably rewarded by anything more than the honour which will be paid to it in the memory of man. Here the outlook of Thucydides seems to have been akin to that of Sophocles, whatever may or may not have been the differences between their religious beliefs.

Thucydides is our clearest guide to the history and to the thought of the fifth century. His work, like that of the poets, has many aspects. It may be that one of the most important of these is expressed in the last words attributed to Nicias. He encourages his broken army to make a last and a desperate effort:

'If you escape the enemy now, you will all see again the homes for which you long, and the Athenians among you will build up again the great power of Athens, fallen though it is'. And his final sentence, which we must believe was deeply felt by the historian himself, is an adaptation of some lines from Sophocles' *Oedipus Tyrannus*, seen on the stage a quarter of a century before this rapidly approaching disaster: 'It is men who make the city, and not walls or ships with no men inside them.' Though Thucydides would have been the last to minimise the importance of walls and ships.

Woman seated on a tomb, c.400

ARISTOPHANES

WAR AND PEACE

Aristophanes, whose dates are c.450–c.385, was younger than any of the writers so
far considered and he outlived all of them. The war with Persia had been over thirty
years before his birth; in his boyhood the empire was already established and Pericles
was in power. For almost the whole of his life as a comic dramatist the war with
Sparta was in progress. Aeschylus had played an active part in the proverbial good
old days of Marathon and Salamis; Sophocles and even Euripides could remember
the victories of Cimon and the spirit of a democracy with a pronounced aristocratic
and pro-Spartan trend, which also could be put in the category of the good old days.
Aristophanes knew nothing of this period except by hearsay. His frequent contrasts
between the past and the present, between the purity, toughness, grace and honesty
of the old Marathon-fighters, and the intemperance, laxity, self-seeking individualism
and dishonesty of the present age have all the charm and, historically speaking, much
of the inaccuracy which we associate with nostalgia. But Aristophanes is not a historian. He is that rarest of things, a serious comic poet. He could only have lived
when he did and there has been no one like him since then. His pictures of the past
and the present may be inaccurate in detail. Not all of the generation of Marathon
were wise and good; Pericles did not start the war to satisfy a whim of his mistress,
Aspasia; and it is far from the intention of Aristophanes to persuade us that his fantasy
is fact. And yet his fantasy, even when most extravagant, has a reality of its own. It is
never sentimental, as it often is in Dickens, who in sheer exuberance does almost
rival Aristophanes and who, like him, very often writes with a serious purpose. Also,
while Dickens, perhaps because of prejudices of his own, perhaps because of the
conventions of his time, is very ill at ease with certain characters – with the upper
class in general, with young heroines and with most things that took place before his
boyhood – Aristophanes has a sure and certain touch with all his creations. He
is at ease with all his characters and caricatures of every age, of every class, male
or female, human or divine. Jurymen, politicians, generals, poets, housewives, philosophers, intellectuals and anti-intellectuals, imaginary political birds of every species
– they are all, in whatever situation, whether fantastical or realistic, bursting with

Terracotta statuettes of actors

vitality and treated with a zest that continues until the very end of the war, through the darkest days. Then the vitality ebbs, the zest goes. Comedy, in the old spacious sense, like tragedy, has come to an end.

Singing and dancing must have been the original raw material of comedy as they were of tragedy, but, as the word implies, comedy is the singing of a band of revellers, a *kômos*. The particular *kômos* seems usually to have been associated with fertility cults and was no doubt very ancient and very widespread. Vase paintings of the sixth century from Sparta and Corinth as well as Athens show wild dances with the dancers often dressed up as animals and often equipped with an exaggerated phallus; and in the developed Attic comedy a phallus was part of the equipment of the chorus, often a purely conventional part which would probably pass unnoticed by the audience except in some farcical scenes where it might be important. Another ancient element which remains incorporated in the developed Attic comedy is the final scene which always contains some form of wedding or sexual union, though this scene also may have little bearing on the rest of the play.

However mere revelry, sacred or profane, high spirits, fertility rites and more or less licentious dancing are not sufficient to make a play. For this there are required characterization and some form of a plot. These elements seem to have come, in the case of comedy, though not of tragedy, which developed independently, to mainland Greece from Sicily and, when incorporated with the old predominately phallic *kômos*, formed something quite new.

Epicharmus of Syracuse (c. 530–440) seems to have written clever, literary plays which were quite short and which (to judge from the titles and the few fragments which have come down to us) ranged over a variety of subjects. Stories about the gods are treated wittily and irreverently. Poseidon, for instance, is represented as a fishmonger and Heracles is already established in his role of a colossal eater. More important, the plays are written in a style which presupposes an educated literary audience who are interested in contemporary events and fashions and ways of thought. There is a definite plot and there are typical characters from everyday life.

In Attic comedy there are elements from both the indigenous phallic procession, with its total freedom of speech, dance and song, delight in exaggeration and irresponsible knock-about fun, and also from the more carefully constructed and topical Sicilian productions. It may be because this blend of styles took longer to reach a more or less definite form that comedy was officially recognised by the state later than tragedy. It was not until 486 that contests in comedy were held at the Great Dionysia in March, and not until about 440 that they were included in the other dramatic festival of the Lenaea in January.

To judge from the eleven complete plays of Aristophanes and from what is known of the plots of the other comic writers, the form of this Old Comedy varied only slightly from play to play. First comes the prologue, which introduces the plot (which may be a very thin one); then, after the entrance of the chorus, comes an *agôn* or contest between two opposite principles or points of view – the new education versus the old education, women versus men, peace versus war. Then comes the *parabasis*, a long address made directly to the audience by the chorus. Here the chorus usually speaks for the author and gives his comments on political events, on personalities or on questions of literary style. The only form of censorship by which the author seems to feel himself constrained is in his sense of how much the audience will stand. Thus his serious political themes, or his complaints about how the audience have had the bad taste to prefer other dramatists to him, are put in a way likely to arouse sympathetic laughter rather than antagonism. He is not afraid, in fact he is expected to attack the leading and popular figures of the day in terms which, if used in any other period of history, would certainly lead to the suppression of the play and to very unpleasant consequences to its author.

After this long, varied and free-ranging commentary on events, which need have little or nothing to do with the plot of the play, comes a series of episodes in which the leading character deals drastically with various unwelcome types of character from contemporary life – a tax-collector, an informer, a war-mongering general – usually people who attempt, but fail, to get a share in the good things of life which the hero, by various expedients, has secured for himself and for all good like-minded citizens. And the play ends with the final jollification of a revel and some kind of a marriage.

Within this general structure there is room for all kinds of variations and some-times, though not often, there is a change in the order of the parts. In the *Frogs*, for instance, the *agôn*, in this case the literary contest between the very substantial shades of Aeschylus and Euripides, comes near the end of the play. But, though the structure is comparatively loose, it is important. It provides a framework within which the playwright can exercise some control over the bursting exuberance of his fantasy and in which the audience, who will never know quite what to expect next, will at least be familiar with a certain pattern that will be followed.

As is evident, development of plot and character is not important, as it is in tragedy and in all subsequent comedy. What is important is the imaginary situation, which is usually fantastic or impossible, together with the opportunities with which it provides the dramatist to show his skill in farce, in quick character sketches, in social or political satire, in serious political theory, in literary criticism and parody, and in lyric poetry which can represent all moods except the severely tragic.

It may seem surprising that such a farrago of style, incident, character and inten-tion can have a form at all, and indeed the loose conventional structure which has been outlined does not appear to guarantee any greater unity than might be found in a series of English music-hall sketches interspersed with episodes from Gilbert and Sullivan, attacks on individuals which would come under the law of libel, political statements which might remind one of Milton's *Areopagitica*, together with obsceni-ties and knock-about fun concerning the gods of the state religion which would not remind one of Milton at all. Such a wild mixture of disparate elements seems scarcely to deserve the name of art; it appears more suited to the relaxed and unbuttoned entertainment of tired businessmen than to the eager and intellectually appreciative interest of citizens who never give the impression of knowing what tiredness is.

Yet these plays certainly do have a unity of their own, though perhaps it is a unity more difficult for us to grasp and understand than that of Greek tragedy. Much of our difficulty comes from the fact that this type of comedy is unique and quite unlike anything else to which we are accustomed. Greek tragedy, in spite of some elements (such as the part played by the chorus, by music and by dancing) which are strange to us, does not strike us as something utterly new. The same themes and some of the same methods are present in Shakespeare. And one may say, no doubt, that some of the themes, some of the characters and situations of Aristophanes can be paralleled in Shakespeare, in Rabelais and elsewhere. But nothing at all like the whole sweep and totality of Aristophanes and the comic writers of the last half of the fifth century has ever been known since.

It seems fair to attribute this phenomenon to the nature of Athenian democracy itself, which did not last much longer than the tragedy and the comedy which it had produced. Modern theories of participatory democracy and audience participation are not likely to be very helpful, since the participation of the citizen of Athens in both his government and his entertainment was more thorough and complete and at the same time more strictly bound by convention than anything imagined by modern theorists or possible either in a modern representative assembly or in a modern theatre.

The freedom of speech, or *parrhesia*, on which the Athenians so prided themselves was exercised within limits. Insulting words or behaviour, particularly when they occurred in public, whether directed against a fellow-citizen, a foreigner or a slave, might render one liable to severe legal penalties. This kind of insult was a blow to another's self-respect and was regarded as an offence against the whole community. And in public life, while there was nothing to stop any citizen from rising to great power so long as he had a sufficient number of supporters, his actions were still subject to all kinds of checks and scrutinies from committees chosen by lot and possibly hostile to him. And in this close and often severe control exercised over politicians, generals and other officials every citizen played a part. It was not important to feel that the individual *ought* to share in government. He *had* to share in it and, as a rule, he prided himself on it. Moreover this democratic supervision, wisely or unwisely, could extend very far. Not only were the actions and policies of public officials subject to review, control or condemnation. The jurymen who from all walks of life served in the law courts could investigate what would now be considered a man's personal and private beliefs. This, admittedly, did not often happen, but, as we have seen, it happened in the cases of Phidias, Anaxagoras and others and, after the turn of the century in what were certainly exceptional circumstances, one of the greatest and most patriotic of all Athenians, Socrates, was to be put to death, not for any action he had done, but because he was regarded as a dangerous moral influence.

Thus, though Pericles and the Athenians generally, prided themselves on the freedom and ease of their way of life – something not to be found in Sparta or indeed anywhere else – it is evident that this very real freedom was far from being irresponsible and was exercised within limits not all of which we should find tolerable.

The Old Comedy may appear at first sight to have escaped entirely from the conventions and restrictions which were present in social and political life and also present in tragedy. But comedy, like tragedy, has its origins in religion and ritual and these origins are, in some ways, more evident in the apparent licence and irresponsibility of comedy than they are in tragedy. Tragedy very soon freed itself from the mere choric description or glorification of the doings of gods or heroes. Though it retained its serious and even religious tone, though its performances were always part of a religious festival, its main concern was with the moral conflicts of men and only with gods in so far as their presumed action or inaction concerned men. These men may be magnified or intensified by poetry or by situation, but they are all recognisable in contemporary terms. Their problems are great ones, and they are treated with the greatest seriousness; but they are problems which all men, in whatever period of history they may be living, may have to face. And, except in the late romantic plays of Euripides, they must be taken and treated with the seriousness that they deserve. In developed tragedy there is very little of that ecstatic and otherworldly element which may have been prominent in its very early days and when it does appear, as in Euripides' *Bacchae*, it results in something which, however powerful, is strangely and alarmingly inhuman.

In Old Comedy, however, the original ecstatic element has not only survived but is always of the greatest importance. It also has become humanized, but it is humanized in precisely the opposite way to that which we find in tragedy. In tragedy we follow the fortunes and decisions of great men and great situations, but we shall be unmoved unless these great men and situations are not only possible, but so life-like that we, even on a humbler scale, can feel as these heroes feel. But in comedy there are no great men (or, if there are, they are parodied or caricatured) and the situations are not only improbable but often totally impossible. Much of the ecstasy which, we assume, marked the early fertility rites and revels remains, but it is of a form which can scarcely be called religious. The restraints which must be present in ordinary social and political life are certainly relaxed but they are not entirely abolished. The result of the freedom from inhibitions is not an identification with the divine but rather a delightful wish-fulfilment of the most ordinary and normal desires. The ambitions to be gratified are not for power or virtue or wisdom; they are for plenty of food and drink, for sex and for the end of the war.

The essence of this comedy is in the uninhibited laughter of the ordinary sensual man; but since this ordinary man happens to be an Athenian, who is always political, always questioning, always on some sort of service, military or civil, there are more elements than this. In Aristophanes we find detailed literary criticism, very often in the form of parodies of Euripides, violent political attacks, notably on Cleon, and sometimes a kind of comedy of escape into impossible Utopias. But even the Utopias are political. They may be built in the clouds with the aid of the birds and be able to defy gods and men, but they will always be strangely like Athens, only with all abuses miraculously removed and with plenty of the good things of life to be enjoyed by all good citizens. The feasting and the marriage with which the plays end point

OVERLEAF: *The largest and finest of Greek theatres, that at Epidaurus could seat over 7000 people and had unsurpassed natural acoustics.*

to the wished-for satisfaction of an impossible world of happy-ever-after and we share gratefully and hilariously in the sensual delight. But on the way to this conclusion there has been pointed criticism and invective concerned with contemporary personalities, trends of thought and political events. From one point of view the play may be seen as wholly fantastic, from another as wholly and piercingly relevant. But we shall fail to see the point of this comedy if we emphasise one aspect at the expense of the other. The knock-about fun, the wildly improbable and funny situations are not there in order to make palatable some healthy, though bitter, medicine of a relevant message. The message is in the laughter and the laughter is in the message. They go hand in hand.

The fact that Aristophanes must have his audience with him from the beginning of a play to the end, laughing when he laughs, listening when he is being serious, does not, of course, mean that he must be a slave to public opinion or avoid expressing ideas which are not generally accepted. To speak or write to please the people was always something which the speaker or writer claimed that he would never do, though no doubt in practice he often did so. The poet, in particular, was expected to say something worth hearing, out of the ordinary and likely to make men better. And an Athenian audience liked, above all things, to hear an argument. To say what everybody thought obvious would be to them inexpressibly boring. We know, for instance, that the Athenians were as patriotic as anyone has ever been, yet we have no record of a single patriotic play. The one apparent exception, Aeschylus' *Persians*, is concerned more with the humiliation of the pride of Xerxes than with the glory of Salamis. On the other hand we cannot imagine that an Athenian audience would have sat through a play which was thoroughly unpatriotic. Great as was an author's freedom of speech on the stage, there were some things which he could not say. There were occasions in Athenian history when a speaker who, in desperate circumstances, had proposed surrendering to the enemy had been stoned to death.

Aristophanes was a brave man, as is shown by his attacks on Cleon which resulted in some form of prosecution, but he was not a fool and he understood both the temper of his audience and the nature of his art. To attack important political figures on the comic stage did not imply courage, though it may have done so in the case of Cleon. Comic writers had attacked Pericles for years. And in order to explain this Athenian practice of abusing well-known figures on the stage it is unnecessary to resort to theories showing that abuse of the great was held to be a charm against the envy of the gods or the evil eye. Such beliefs may have played a part in the Roman habit of singing scurrilous verses about a general at the time of his triumph or in the uninhibited songs sung at weddings. For Athenian comedy it is sufficient to point to the obvious fact that to make fun of a character whom nobody has ever heard of is not amusing. We laugh when the rich, the pompous, the distinguished or the opinionated come to grief on the stage. We should not laugh at seeing the same ludicrous mishaps occurring to children or to poor old women.

And in Athens the enormous political and moral freedom of the comic writer, while it served the useful social purpose of providing a safety valve for those feelings of discontent and dissatisfaction which are normally restrained in everyday life, was firmly based on laughter and, since it assumed a real spirit of community in the audience, was never purely factional or embittered. One could laugh at seeing statesmen, poets or philosophers in absurd and humiliating situations and still, on the next day, vote for the statesmen and applaud the poets or philosophers.

It goes without saying that Aristophanes, like his fellow-citizens, had definite ideas on a number of subjects, but they are not at all easy to state clearly. It does appear that he really disliked Cleon and that he was opposed to Cleon's tyrannical treatment of the allies. Perhaps his most violent attack on this demagogue was made in the *Knights*, produced in 424 when Cleon was at the height of his popularity. In this play two generals who were much in the public eye, Nicias and Demosthenes, appear as slaves of an old man, Demos (the people of Athens). The two slaves complain of the harsh treatment they are getting from their master's favourite, a Paphlagonian, who is a caricature of Cleon. Nicias is represented, though in exaggerated terms, as being recognisably like the real person – god-fearing, honest, cautious to the point of timidity. The brilliant general Demosthenes is quick and resolute and rather too fond of the bottle. Cleon is a vulgar, violent, uneducated bully. In the end, after a lot of farcical actions, Cleon is supplanted in his master's favour by a character, the Offal-Seller, who unbelievably is able to excel him in all his own vices. One might think that poor old Demos, under the influence of a man who is more violent, more boastful and uncouth than Cleon himself, has now got himself into quite a hopeless situation. But not at all. Aristophanes can break through all the shackles of common sense and probability as easily as can any writer of space fiction. The Offal-Seller suddenly, and quite unaccountably, turns out to be a great and high-minded deliverer. His skill in magic enables him to rejuvenate Demos, and in the place of the gullible and corrupt old man we see to our delight, fresh and youthful, the Athens of old, 'shining Athens, the violet-crowned', pure, strong and uncorrupted, as she was in the days of Marathon.

No doubt the audience applauded this final piece of wishful thinking which would gratify their national pride and fill them with a sense, however illusory, that all could still turn out well. But they must also have applauded the rest of the play and laughed at the disrespectful treatment given to important characters, each of whom must have had a large following among the spectators. There would be many who at this time would be loud in their praises of Cleon for his recent success at Pylos where, for the first time in known history, crack Spartan troops had surrendered their arms. Others, with considerable reason, would argue that this victory had been won, not by Cleon, who was claiming all the credit, but by the bold and skilful generalship of Demosthenes. And there would be still others who were loyal and devoted supporters of the good and respected Nicias, who hated and despised Cleon and had won more victories than anyone living.

It is unlikely that any of the three statesmen much enjoyed the jokes made at their expense and Cleon, in particular, may have been greatly angered. But the audience, sections of which in ordinary life would have eagerly defended one or other of the generals and attacked the remaining two, seem to have been delighted to see all three made to look ludicrous or worse in the theatre. One may say with truth that the laughter of comedy is a welcome, if temporary, relief from the strenuousness of serious political life, that it is a healthy pleasure to escape into an imaginary world where what could never happen does happen and where things are said and done which, in a way, one would like to do and say oneself, though in normal life one is prevented from doing so by fear, by good manners or by the exigencies of fact. But what is really surprising is the spirit of unanimity and good fellowship which allowed a people so politically conscious and often so violent in its partisan or factional feeling to join together in enjoyment of a spectacle in which, at some moment or other, almost every man's pet theories, favourite speakers or cherished convictions would be made to look very foolish indeed.

This feeling of unanimity, of comradeship, of being, whatever might be said, really all good friends together may have been helped by the convention of the comic stage. It was known that the play would end in general merry-making where everyone would be happy and contented. But the tact of the dramatist must also have played a large part. One could and should say a great many things that could not be said in the convention of ordinary social and political life; but these things had to be said in a certain way and with a certain tone. And there still remained some things that could not be said at all.

Among these things would be a serious plea for making peace with Sparta on Sparta's terms. Aristophanes has often been admired for his so-called pacifism. The admiration is mistaken. In the Athens he knew such a thing as pacifism was unknown and unthought of. One could and did dislike the war intensely and one would be ready, as all soldiers have always been ready, to grumble at the incapacity of generals and politicians. But for anyone to maintain that his conscience or his moral sense forbade him to take part in a war in which his city was involved would be unthinkable. He might try to avoid military service by various expedients, but the expedient or the faith of a conscientious objector was simply not open to him.

Aristophanes wrote several plays (notably the *Acharnians* in 425) in which the main theme is the desirability of peace in contrast to the miseries of war. In these plays there are attacks both on the policy which led to the war and on the generals and politicians who are carrying it on or are unnecessarily prolonging it. And it is true that at no other period of history would such attacks have been tolerated on the stage of any country which was engaged in a life and death struggle with a powerful enemy. But this fact does not in any way imply that Aristophanes was engaged in what we should call anti-war propaganda or that, if he had been doing so, his audience would have allowed him to continue. In all the attacks, most of which are light-hearted and fantastic, on individual war-mongers and on particular policies and in all the praises of the delights of peace there is never any hint of a suggestion that Athens is fighting an unjust war and that Sparta is in the right. One may be free to assume that all the politicians on both sides are fools or worse, but never that those from Athens are inferior to those from Sparta. Indeed in any fantastic wish-fulfilment of a return to peace and plenty that may be devised, the initiative is always Athenian.

In the *Acharnians* the leading figure is an old countryman, Dicaeopolis, who decides on the impossible plan of making a separate peace with Sparta. He is opposed first by his own villagers, tough old vinegrowers who have seen their vines destroyed by the Spartan invaders, and then by the war-loving general Lamachus. The old villagers are treated sympathetically, as are all such people in Aristophanes; the general is made to look ridiculous in a number of farcical accidents. Once he has surmounted these obstacles Dicaeopolis begins to enjoy his separate peace by trading with the enemy. A starving citizen of the neighbouring state of Megara, which has been yearly ravaged by Athenian armies and is cut off from all trade with Athens and her allies, attempts to sell him his two small children done up in a bag and pretending to be sucking-pigs. Then a man from the rich agricultural area of Boeotia arrives. He has to offer everything of which the Athenians have been deprived by the war – every variety of game and poultry and the favourite Athenian dish of eels from Lake Copais. Dicaeopolis is short of money, but the Boeotian wants in return for all these good things something that is really and specifically Attic. So Dicaeopolis pays him with an informer, who is trussed up and stuffed into a bag. The play ends with the usual feasting and merriment. The good are all happy and the bad are turned away from the feast. Dicaeopolis, already slightly drunk, is enjoying every moment.

In the course of the play there have been a number of very loosely connected and farcical incidents. There is an envoy from Persia who is much more interested in getting money out of the Athenians for himself than in giving them any help. There are some outlandish Thracians with their absurd dialect who are most unlikely to be any use as allies. There is a farcical account of the origins of the war which no one could possibly take seriously, but which might certainly raise, though in a fantastic and light-hearted way, the question: 'After all, what's it all for?'

Such questions, together with a longing for peace and bright imaginary pictures of how one will then enjoy oneself, are common to most soldiers and certainly do not imply a willingness to mutiny or to surrender to the enemy. The fact that the Athenians could tolerate the expression of these feelings on the stage indicates not that they were willing to listen to 'minority opinion' or to dangerous and disruptive views, but rather that they were prepared to listen to anything, so long as it was not put too seriously. The point is well put by Bowra, who writes:[1]

> [Aristophanes] was not a pacifist at all, but an ordinary man who released all the complaints and fancies which soldiers on active service indulge. His triumph is that he makes them all hilariously funny, and for that reason alone he must not be treated as a solemn advocate of peace at all costs. His strength is that in the middle of war he can treat it with these high spirits, and the strength of the Athenians was that they could share his feelings and enjoy what he said and yet continue to fight with the same persistence as before.

The *Peace* was produced in a different atmosphere. At the time the Athenians could really believe that the war was over and in fact the so-called Peace of Nicias

[1] *Landmarks in Greek Literature*, p. 197

was signed shortly after the performance of Aristophanes' play. The peace was neither real nor lasting. Each side could complain that the other had failed to fulfil some conditions of the treaty and hostilities soon began again. But at the time prospects seemed good. The two chief proponents of war, the Athenian Cleon and the Spartan Brasidas, had been killed the previous year. The invasions of Attica, which had come almost every year, ceased and there seemed every reason for a celebration of joy and relief. The play ends with the marriage of the hero, Trygaeus, a plain, blunt, but very shrewd Athenian, to the oppressed maiden, Peace, and all the Greek cities dance in joy around the happy pair.

But the ravages and miseries of war, the dislocation of all conventions and pieties, also receive their treatment. The cities indeed dance round Trygaeus and his bride, but their dancing is handicapped by the fact that they are all wounded and limping, bandaged or on crutches. And before the happy consummation it has been shown that the whole world is out of joint. Trygaeus has had the bright idea of flying to Olympus on a dung beetle in order to get direct help from the gods; but when he

Terracotta statuettes of actors

arrives, he finds that things are as bad in heaven as they are on earth. The gods also are short of food. In their despair they have handed over everything to the most savage among them, War, and have themselves simply got out of the way. War has buried Peace in a deep pit and has just gone out to supply himself with a new pestle for the purpose of pounding up all the cities in a mortar. Trygaeus succeeds in persuading the cities to join together in pulling Peace out of the pit, but there are still difficulties to be overcome: the Argives, who, as neutrals have been making profits out of both sides, will not do their share of work; the starving Megarians simply lack the strength to pull on the rope; those Spartans who want peace most are the ones taken prisoner by the Athenians at Pylos and so are not available; many of the Athenians are so distracted by their constant law-suits that they are useless, and at one point Lamachus is discovered to be sitting on the rope.

However, Peace is delivered at last and everyone is delighted except the war-mongers, the profiteers and the informers. Trygaeus can look forward again to his beloved vines and, after the wedding feast, to the normal good life of the country.

Peace is not the main theme of the *Birds*, but it is an important one. The play was produced in 414, the year in which the great Athenian expedition set out to conquer Sicily. It was a year of the most ambitious and reckless hopes, all of which were to be utterly disappointed, and it was also the year in which the Athenians got into one of their rare states of mass hysteria because of the mutilation of the Hermae and the rumours, for which there seems to have been no foundation, of an aristocratic plot to overthrow the democracy. In this year of so much violent political and imperialistic feeling Aristophanes seems to be looking in another and quite different direction. His play is one of pure and delightful fantasy. Two Athenians, Euelpides and Pistheteros, want to find somewhere where they can live in peace. They ally themselves with the birds and found a city in the sky – Cloud-Cuckoo-Land – where they can not only be independent of, but can dictate to gods and men. There are the usual vain and amusing attempts of various unworthy characters to have a share in the good things, but there is less of politics in this play than in any of the others and more of pure poetry. The conventional good things – food, drink, freedom from constraint – are there in abundance, but these are often transcended in a clear and confident lyricism. The birds are not 'blithe spirits'; like everything in comedy, they are too human for that; but they are the birds of Attica, even of the ideal Attica, companions of the nightingales in the grove of Colonus.

The situation in 411, when Aristophanes produced his *Lysistrata*, was a very different one. The great forces sent to Sicily had been destroyed; important areas of the empire were in revolt; the yearly invasions had been renewed and there was now a permanent Spartan force behind fortifications within a few miles of Athens herself. Still the city held on and, apparently hopeless as the situation was, she still won victories. No Athenian who valued his life would have dreamed of proposing capitulation to Sparta and her allies. And Aristophanes' play of course makes no such suggestion, although his plea for peace, expressed as usual in a fantastic and impossible setting, is real and deeply felt.

He imagines a situation where the women on both sides, who have suffered as much from the war as anyone else, agree, under the influence of the Athenian woman, Lysistrata, to refuse to sleep with their husbands until the men on both sides have enough sense to stop fighting and to return to normal life again. The plot is brilliantly handled and every advantage is taken of its farcical possibilities – the agonies of sexual frustration in the men, the difficulties which Lysistrata has in keeping the women as chaste as they have promised to be and the final happiness of both sexes when peace is made, common sense prevails and they are free to live naturally again.

The fact that women play such an important part and that Lysistrata herself is one of the most impressive figures in all comedy does not, of course, indicate that Aristophanes was a feminist or remotely interested in Women's Liberation. The Athenian women seem to have been perfectly well able to look after themselves without the vote and it is difficult to see how there arose the notion, still often held, that they were ever an oppressed class of mouse-like creatures somehow resembling the more insipid of Dickens' heroines. Certainly the women presented on the Athenian stage, whether comic, like Lysistrata, or tragic, like Clytemnestra or Antigone, are so far from being insipid that they are at least as impressive as any of the men; and this is, after all, what anyone who has ever met an Athenian woman would imagine would be the case.

In none of the plays of Aristophanes in which peace is advocated is there anything which can be called revolutionary or politically anarchic. That Aristophanes preferred peace to war is evident, but so did nearly the whole of his audience. The comedy, with all its realism and with all its wild fantasy, is not divisive; it is rather, by means often of the central struggle or 'agon', an expression of a basic unanimity, a glad acceptance of those things upon which everyone can agree. To assume that the poet was writing for a peace party when he created Dicaeopolis or for a Womens' Liberation Front in the *Lysistrata* is as absurd as it would be to suggest that the *Birds*, with its detailed knowledge of ornithology, was addressed to an audience of eager and earnest bird-watchers.

In all this comedy there is, and must be, a glorification of the normal, even though everyone in the audience knows that he is not living in normal times. It is indeed an imagined and nostalgic normality that is glorified and exalted in situations which, as a moment's thought would tell us, are impossible. But still we are encouraged to muse: 'If only we could all make a separate peace . . . if only the farmers could go back to the fields and our families be united and happy . . . if only we could eat and drink and make love on a tremendous scale without anyone feeling the worse for it . . . if only everything in our city was great and glorious, as in the old days . . . if only the young could behave themselves and the old could be more tolerant!' And in the excitement and laughter of a fast-moving and brilliant drama, we almost believe that it is all true.

The enjoyment demands a certain unanimity and the unanimity implies the consciousness of being in a community with a long and splendid past. Such feelings have often led to a rigid conservatism and to racial and doctrinal intolerance. The Athenians were not immune from these tendencies. In the comedies there are plenty of jokes about the uncouth or ridiculous ways of foreigners, and eccentric or 'advanced' thinkers, like Socrates and Euripides, are made into figures of fun. But it will be a sad thing if it ever happens that we are not allowed to make fun of foreigners and of our neighbours. Usually the ability to do so is a sign of affection and even a bond of unity. The national characteristics attributed by popular and traditional humour to the English, the Scots, the Welsh and the Irish, however unjust, are enjoyed by all, and in Aristophanes' characterizations of the different states of Greece what is remarkable is that there is so little bitterness and so much insistence on a Pan-Hellenic ideal which, however disrupted by war, still exists. We shall refer later to his treatment of Socrates. As for Euripides, along with the ordinary jokes about his new-fangled lyricism, his realistic costumes and his over-subtlety in thought, there is much keen criticism; but there is also a very evident admiration for his poetry, most of which Aristophanes seems to have known by heart. In its combination of tolerance and intolerance, of the conservative with the utterly liberal, this unique comedy, like so much else in the century, baffles definition.

Two girls playing knucklebones

SOCRATES

THE END AND THE BEGINNING

Thanks to the literature which has survived, we are well informed about the events, the political trends, the ways of thought and the divergent interests of this great century. Sculpture and, even more, the paintings on vases enable us to see the amusements and some of the life of the people of whom we read, and the comedies of Aristophanes are packed with the richness and the variety of ordinary living. But with regard to the great men, the men who were not ordinary, we know hardly any of the things which a modern biographer would like to record or a modern reader would like to learn. Indeed any moderately competent journalist, had he been available, could tell us in a few hundred words more about the appearance, manners, personal tastes, friendships and idiosyncrasies of Pericles, Sophocles and the rest than Thucydides or any other great writer of the times has thought fit or interesting to reveal. Even Aristophanes does not help us much here. A caricature, if it is to have any point, must certainly bear some resemblance to its original, but its comic effect will come from the wild exaggeration of a particular feature or the placing of a recognisable character in some utterly impossible situation. On a modern stage a crown and a little stage property could easily make an actress appear like Queen Elizabeth II of England, but if she were then to proceed to order the decapitation of her Prime Minister, we should be wrong to assume that the present monarch had either the power or the faintest inclination to do such a thing, nor, from this flight of fancy, would we be able at all to imagine what she was really like. In a sense Aristophanes gives us more information about the audience than about the characters to which they are expected to react. We know, for instance, that a poet who is always shifting from one disguise to another, is clever with paradoxes and who sings beautiful and rather meaningless lyrics was readily taken as a representation of Euripides and that an eccentric kind of person, an ascetic and a dealer in subtle logical distinctions, raised above the earth in a basket so that his thoughts might be less earthbound, could be taken to be Socrates. This shows us that the audience were familiar with the plots, the lyrical innovation and some of the mannerisms of Euripides and that Socrates, a quarter of a century before his death, was well known and thought to be a philo-

Socrates, 'as ugly as a mask of Silenus, but somehow after a bit you began to find him beautiful'

sopher mainly interested in natural science, though with some eccentricities of his own. But of the real characters of Euripides and Socrates or even of what Aristophanes really thought of them we learn little or nothing from these displays. As for Pericles, the most prominent man of his time, all the comic writers can tell us is that he had a dignity of speech and manner, that he was fond of Aspasia and that he had a curiously shaped head.

In the whole century only one man has been revealed to us in his personal appearance, his manners, his gestures, his intimate thoughts and feelings. That man is Socrates, who, without having written a word, is more widely known and remembered than any of his contemporaries and has exercised at least as great an influence on all subsequent history. Of Socrates we have much more than a clear picture. We seem to be able not only to see him in front of us, but to hear his voice, watch his movements and feel his touch. The contradictory elements in him, so far from confusing us, only make him seem the more real. And he, perhaps more than any other historical character, is still capable of arousing the emotions proper to real life. Centuries after his death he has been loved or hated with the same passion as he was in his own life; and though the love and veneration in which Erasmus held him and the hatred which he aroused in Nietzsche differ from the feelings of Plato on the one hand or of those who condemned him to death on the other, the feelings are equally intense.

Socrates and Plato

The reality which he still has in our eyes is due, in the first place, to his own reality and after that to the devotion, the sensitivity and the astonishing literary and dramatic genius of Plato. The dramatic dialogue was a new form, invented by Plato and employed in the first place simply to tell people what Socrates was really like. It was natural for him to begin by showing how unjust had been the sentence which had condemned his master to death. This aim might have been achieved merely by argument and by the explanation of prejudices. But Plato, though he is certainly not averse from argument, did not choose these methods. After all one argument could always be countered by another and, as we shall see, the accusers of Socrates did have one or two arguments which, though specious, could certainly be made to look convincing. But to Plato there was one argument which must be totally and without question convincing, an argument which would command not only intellectual approval and assent, but the assent and certainty of the whole personality. This was to be found not so much in what Socrates may have said on this or that occasion but in what Socrates was throughout his whole life. He had been condemned for not believing in the gods in which the city believed and for corrupting the youth. The charges could be answered easily enough; but if one could see Socrates plain, one would see, so clearly as to make such mistakes impossible, a man who believed more firmly and devoutly in the gods than any of his fellow-citizens, a man whose reverence for the laws was as great or greater even than that of Pericles, a man whose whole life had been devoted not to the corruption, but to the purification and ennobling of the youth. And this man, far from having been a somewhat remote, if edifying, figure, had possessed in a supreme degree just those qualities which Athenians most admired – wit, brilliance, curiosity, charm, immense physical endurance, the ability to get on with anyone. He was as ugly as a mask of Silenus, but somehow after a bit one began to find him beautiful; he had a shambling kind of walk, but was immensely strong; he was indifferent to food and drink, but could drink Alcibiades under the table without turning a hair. He was the best friend and the best man that anyone had ever known.

This personality is presented to us by Plato with utter conviction and with consummate skill and tact. And in the portrait which Xenophon gives us of the same man there is nothing inconsistent with Plato's account, so long as we remember that Plato was a more sensitive observer and probably a more intimate disciple of the master than was Xenophon. Plato was too young to have known Socrates until the last years of his life, but for at least some of these years he evidently knew him well and in his uncles, Charmides and Critias, he had others who had known him since their youth. Xenophon did not know him for so long and was away in Asia with the famous ten thousand mercenaries at the time of his trial and condemnation and death. Moreover, although Xenophon was a brilliant commander, a magnificent story-teller and a person of great charm and much sense, he was not a philosopher nor a political theorist of any distinction. That his account of the personality and the basic teachings of Socrates differs so little, except in emphasis and in literary dexterity, from that of Plato is testimony to Plato's own accuracy. It is difficult any longer to believe that in Xenophon we have the real Socrates which can be opposed to a largely fictitious Socrates used by Plato as a mouthpiece for his own ideas.[1]

Socrates himself, according to Plato, saw clearly at the time of his trial that the real danger confronting him was not in any specific charge that could be made against

[1]An excellent and, to my mind, entirely convincing discussion of this problem is to be found in the third volume of *A History of Greek Philosophy*, W. K. C. Guthrie. Cambridge, 1969.

him, but rather in a general prejudice based on lack of knowledge and leading to a total misunderstanding of his real aims. It would be easy enough to show that a man with a military record like his could not be fairly accused of being unpatriotic or that a man so god-fearing could not be seriously regarded as an atheist. Much more difficult to meet was the charge that, whatever Socrates' beliefs or actions might have been, his general influence had been socially and politically disruptive and pernicious.

In attempting to controvert this charge, or this prejudice, both Plato and Xenophon are concerned to mark the distinction between Socrates and the great sophists of the day, Protagoras, Gorgias and Prodicus. Plato shows much more sympathy with and understanding of these men than Xenophon does and, largely because of this, is able to demonstrate that, while there are some similarities between their methods and those of Socrates, there is a basic difference much more profound and complete than is evident to Xenophon. What, with all his skill and understanding, he does not demonstrate is that, from the point of view of an Athenian democrat, Socrates was not much more politically dangerous than any sophist.

The great sophists, who reached the height of their popularity in the years before Plato was born and during his childhood, were, according to the standards of the fifth century, eminently practical men. They charged fees for their lectures or for their instruction and this is the point of difference between them and Socrates which is most often mentioned by Socrates' supporters. But they would certainly claim that they gave value for the money which they received. Plato himself never presents them as charlatans. Some of the less well known of them, like Thrasymachus in the *Republic*, are represented as rude and bad-tempered if they get the worst of an argument. But on the whole they are treated with respect. They may be shown to be a little pompous or conceited, but all this is done with wit and with good nature. Socrates respects their genuine learning and is interested in their search for the correct use of language just as Pericles had been. Nor can he possibly object to payment being given for services rendered. In the unspecified times when he was either employed or self-employed as a worker in stone (which can mean anything from a stone-mason to a sculptor like Phidias) he must have received payment himself from others. His quarrel with them goes much deeper than the matter of taking wages for what they have to offer. What he is really attacking is the whole basis on which they work and on which their work is accepted. And this attack, couched in the most polite and considerate language, in a manner of exquisite charm and understanding, is in fact an utterly revolutionary attack on the underlying principles of Periclean democracy.

That the sophists were able to purvey useful knowledge of grammar, mathematics, anthropology and much else, Socrates would not dispute for a moment. What he objects to is their claim to be able to impart the learning and skill which would prove useful to an ambitious man in political life. Yet to no one except Socrates did there seem to be anything wrong with this aim. At no period has the power of the spoken word been so effective as it was in Socrates' life-time. It was natural and proper for every man to learn to speak as well and as convincingly as possible, and, in the view of Pericles and many others, the whole health and strength of the city depended on free discussion; only after the expression of different points of view could one choose the best course of action to take. It was, of course, admitted that bad advice might be given and, if given persuasively enough, might be taken. The drama of the time is full of warnings against 'too persuasive speakers' who may lead a city or an individual into making the wrong decisions. And it is almost always assumed or stated that these evil counsellors are actuated by a desire for personal gain. They may be charged with taking bribes or with plotting to establish a tyranny; seldom or never is their fault attributed to sheer incompetence. In the Periclean scheme of things two articles of faith are taken for granted: one is that every citizen has not only the right, but the duty to express himself on public affairs; the other is that this expression of opinion and its discussion is likely or certain to be valuable to the general well-being of the state and so of every individual citizen.

To both these articles of faith Socrates is firmly and radically opposed; and his opposition is based on a view of the individual and of the state which, while it has grown up in and been fostered by the Periclean age, in fact contradicts the whole theory and practice which has made that age possible.

Pericles, as we have seen, had a faith in human nature and particularly in Athenian nature which in many respects seems almost unbounded. An expression of this faith is put by Thucydides[1] into the mouths of enemies, the Corinthian envoys at Sparta, who say of the Athenians:

> As for their bodies, they regard them as expendable for their city's sake, as though they were not their own; but each man cultivates his own intelligence, again with a view to doing something notable for his city.

Socrates in the course of his life gave ample proof that he was fully able to meet the first of these requirements; he was remarkable too for 'cultivating his intelligence' and he would certainly claim that in his intellectual activity he was 'doing something notable for his city'. It is in the definition of what precisely is notable that he parts company with Pericles and with all previous Greek thought. The empire, the power, splendour and glory of Athens no doubt meant much to him, but in none of these things, taken by themselves, did he find what to him was really notable. These things were only 'good' or 'useful' (the words are interchangeable) in so far as they promoted the health of the soul.

Nearly all later admirers of Socrates will describe this as a religious attitude and will contrast it with the more mundane or 'lower' attitude of ordinary politics. We in the West are used to believing that the superior values of the City of God, while they may influence and gradually ameliorate the City of Man, can never be fully incorporated in it. While we may regret it, we accept the fact that in private and in public life there are somewhat different moral standards. And even in private life, while idealism, so long as it is not starry-eyed, may be approved, it will still need to be under the control of a realistic attitude.

[1] Thuc. I, 70

Most of these distinctions, if recognised by Socrates at all, appeared to him in a very different form. In particular he would have found it difficult or impossible to understand what we mean by the word 'religious'. No system of religion other than the long and often incoherent tradition of mythology was available to him, and he did not claim for himself any particular inspiration or revelation except for his '*daimonion*' or 'divine sign' which, he said, would warn him sometimes against taking some particular action, but which never gave him any positive instruction. His argument and his whole way of thought is almost entirely intellectual and it is carried on for the most part in the usual terms of the fifth century, terms which would be familiar to Aeschylus, Pericles, Sophocles and Thucydides alike. Like these men and like the sophists he attempted to reach his conclusions by logical argument and he too was concerned with the precise definitions of the words and the terms involved. Aristotle gives Socrates the credit for two important innovations in philosophy – inductive argument and general definition; and he is, of course, entirely right in so far as the Socratic method is concerned. But it is still true that many people before Socrates had found that the use of examples would support their case and that the use of a generally accepted definition might clinch it. Socrates may differ from the rest in showing a greater zeal in testing out each hypothesis or general definition by seeing whether it can be properly applied to every conceivable particular case, and he may show a more than ordinary urgency in his quest for a truth that is incontrovertible. These must be recognised as valuable qualities in a logician, and it is as a logician that Aristotle is discussing Socrates' contribution to philosophy.

But to Plato and Xenophon who, unlike Aristotle, had known Socrates personally, his abilities as a logician, admirable as they were, were not the most important thing about him. They found the real meaning and message and inspiration of his life and personality in something which went rather beyond his love for truth, great as that was and greatly in accordance with everything in him. He could not, they might have said, have loved truth so much, loved he not something else – his friends? Athens? the soul? goodness? – more.

Even Plato, who was as great a logician, as sensitive a man and as accomplished an artist as any who ever lived, never precisely defines what this something more was, although he gives us plenty of hints; and, if Plato cannot exactly define it, it is most unlikely that anyone else will be able to do so. But we may have, perhaps, one advantage over Plato and that is that, with so much more history to look back on, we can see even more clearly than he did how revolutionary the thought of Socrates has turned out to be. Plato, as is natural, sees him clearly as a man of the fifth century and, considering the accusations that were made against him, is concerned to emphasise those established fifth-century virtues of patriotism, piety, courage and justice which he undoubtedly had. And to Plato it was an additional virtue that, instead of being content, like other men, simply to practise these virtues, Socrates was determined also to understand and, if possible, to define them. In so doing, Plato believes, he was conferring a great benefit, perhaps the greatest of all, on his friends, on Athens and on all mankind.

Youth who holds a bird in his left hand and raises his right to a cage. From a gravestone, c.400.

Put like this, few would disagree with Plato's verdict. Much the same, with slight variations, could be said of Aeschylus, Sophocles or Thucydides. But this is not the whole story and Plato is much too honest to desire or attempt to suppress the rest of it. What is really revolutionary about Socrates' life and teaching is not its content but its spirit and its implications. These are personal to a degree unimagined by Pericles or indeed by anyone else before Socrates. In the last resort what is of supreme importance to him is not the health of the city, but the health of the individual soul. He, like Pericles, would no doubt assert that the two go together and interact; but while Pericles will say that where the state as a whole is doing well, there each individual citizen will also be doing well, Socrates would require further explanation. And if by doing well is meant simply or mainly an increase in wealth or power, he would not agree. To the individual soul an excess of wealth or power unjustly used is positively harmful.

About this belief too there does not appear to be, at first sight, anything unusual. All conventional opinion would agree that injustice and excess will lead to trouble and should be avoided. In the latter part of the fifth century, as we have seen, the conventional view had come under attack from some who maintained that justice and injustice and such terms were only words 'according to convention' and that what was real 'according to nature' was the possession and acquisition of power. In attacking such modern ideas, as he did, and in proving that justice and injustice not only mean something but mean something so important that the whole health of the soul depends on following the one and avoiding the other, Socrates might well seem to be performing a useful and indeed a conservative aim. Was not this, after all, just what the old Marathon-fighters, the founders of the democracy, had believed in? If Socrates, notoriously one of the new thinkers, was found to be defending the old morality, agreeing that the laws should be obeyed, that the young should treat their elders with respect, that citizens should work and live together in a spirit of tolerance and forbearance, ready and willing to face hardship and danger when called upon to do so, was not this, though surprising in a modern philosopher, very gratifying and a sign of grace?

But anyone who thought along these lines was in for a rude shock. It soon became clear that while Socrates was indeed defending the conventional values he was doing this in a most unconventional and disturbing way. While he was ready enough to applaud the toughness and the patriotism of the old Marathon-fighters, he would not let matters rest there. He was far from applauding the intelligence of these excellent men and indeed showed unmistakably that, in his opinion, when they made pronouncements, as they were fully entitled to do, on such subjects as virtue and patriotism, they had only the foggiest notion of what they were talking about. Worse still, he was by no means convinced that the democracy which they had created and defended and the empire which their sons had won were so wonderful after all. He had, it was true, shown himself ready to fight for his country when called upon, and had fought with distinction, but in all other respects he was far from being a model citizen. While he was always ready to argue with his friends or anyone else who cared to listen, he took no part in the discussions in the Assembly on public affairs. He had none of the normal political ambition and rather discouraged it in others. He preferred to 'mind his own business', and this, as Pericles had pointed out, was only another way of saying that he had no business to be in Athens at all. His method of defending the 'old' morality seemed to consist in a number of hair-splitting discussions of the meanings of terms which, if it were not for Socrates, everyone could have easily understood, and the end result was that people were less sure of what morality was than they had been in the first place. The fact that Socrates invariably conducted these discussions with impeccable politeness and in the best humour only made matters worse, since in this way good men were made to look even more foolish than they might have looked otherwise. Surely this kind of a defence of morality was at least as dangerous as any overt attack.

And by the time that Socrates came to stand his trial, his accusers could point to facts which were incontrovertible and which were bound to be damaging to him. Among the circle of brilliant young men, often though not always from the best families, the one for whom he had had a particularly great affection was Alcibiades. Plato's uncle, Critias, had been another member of this circle. Nothing about Alcibiades except his personal courage could have possibly commended him to a conventional moralist or democrat. The older members of the jury which condemned Socrates might well have considered that this favourite pupil of his embodied all that had been worst in the younger generation and all that had done most harm to Athens. In his early youth Alcibiades had been renowned not only for his beauty and his great abilities, but for an insatiable ambition, reckless extravagance and a total lack of consideration for other people. He had risen to high office at an unusually early age and had been one of the commanders, as he had been the chief sponsor, of the expedition to Sicily. Before the expedition had achieved anything of importance he had been recalled to Athens to stand his trial on charges of being connected with the profanation of the mysteries and the mutilation of the Hermae, which involved suspicion of plotting to overthrow the democracy and set up a tyranny. Neither at the time nor subsequently has anyone produced any evidence to show that Alcibiades had been guilty of any of these things, but lack of evidence did not prevent the distrust felt of him by almost everyone except his personal friends and the troops under his command. Instead of returning to Athens to face his trial and, he must have considered, his certain condemnation, he had gone over to Sparta and by the advice which he gave there did Athens more harm in the war than any of her enemies had done. In the speech which he made at Sparta, as reported by Thucydides,[1] he attempted, among other things, to dispel any mistrust which the Spartans might feel for him because of his career as a democratic leader and an Athenian patriot. In dealing with the first count, he admits that members of his family (which included Cleisthenes and Pericles) have indeed been leaders of the common people. He claims that they have acted in the interests of 'the state as a whole' – a claim with which Pericles would agree. But his next remarks are of a kind which would have horrified

[1]Thuc. VI, 89

ΗΓΗΣΩ ΠΡΟΞΕΝΟ

Pericles. The only reason, he says, why they supported the democracy was because it happened to be the system 'which had been handed down to us' – a statement which even the Spartans must have known to be demonstrably untrue. And he adds:

> As for democracy, those of us with any sense at all knew what that meant, and I just as much as any. Indeed I am well equipped to make an attack on it; but nothing new can be said of a system which is generally recognised as absurd.

Later in the same speech he defends himself against the charge – a reasonable enough one to make – that in turning against his country and in doing her all the harm he can he is acting like a traitor. His defence is ingenious, if dishonest:

> The Athens I love is not the one which is wronging me now, but the one in which I used to have secure enjoyment of my rights as a citizen . . . And the man who really loves his country is not the one who refuses to attack it when he has been unjustly driven from it, but the man whose desire for it is so strong that he will shrink from nothing in his efforts to get back there again.

Socrates, we may be quite sure, would have utterly dissociated himself from this view of what is meant by loving one's country; but it is by no means certain that he would have dissented from Alcibiades' professed opinion of democracy as being 'generally recognised as absurd'.

At a later period of the war Alcibiades did succeed in getting back to his country and, again in command, won important victories before he was again exiled, and this time too for no fault of his own. But by this time even great victories could never make up the ground which, very largely because of him, had been lost, and when Socrates was on trial, the Alcibiades who would be most remembered was not the brilliant general and diplomatist or the man who had put up a record in winning chariot races at the Olympic games, but the despiser of the common people and the traitor.

The last Athenian fleet had been destroyed in 405 and in the following year Athens had been starved into surrender. The Long Walls built by Pericles had been demolished and the democracy replaced by the government of the Thirty, supported by Spartan troops. The Thirty Tyrants, as they came to be called, had done their best ruthlessly to suppress any opposition and their most able and determined leader had been Critias, another friend and one-time disciple of Socrates. Critias had an open and avowed hatred and contempt for the democracy; he had seized power by assassination and in eight months the Thirty, under his control, had put to death 1,500 citizens and exiled at least 5,000. In 403 the exiled democrats had succeeded in driving out the Thirty and Critias himself had been killed. Considering the sufferings of war and famine, the violent hatred between the oligarchs and the democrats, the failure of ordinary institutions and the numbers of those who had been killed or deprived of their property, Athens appeared to be facing the same kind of total failure as that which Thucydides had described in Corcyra. In fact this was one of the occasions,

Hegeso held a necklace, rendered in paint, which she has taken from the jewelry case proffered by a maid-servant. From a gravestone, c.400

of which there were many, when the faith which Pericles had had in the spirit of the Athenian people and in the validity of the institutions which he had fostered, seemed fully justified, true though it is that Athens was more apt to show her great qualities in times of near disaster than in times of success and prosperity. There was a general political amnesty; the democracy, with the support of all moderate opinion, was re-established; and Athens began rapidly to repair the ruin caused by the war. It was a triumph of good sense and moderation, only marred by the trial and execution of Socrates in 399.

It seems certain that Socrates could easily have escaped death. He could have gone into voluntary exile before the trial, as Anaxagoras had done in another period of anti-intellectualism, or he could, after the verdict, have proposed an alternative penalty less frivolous and less calculated to irritate the jurymen than his proposition that he should, like an Olympic winner, be kept at the public expense for the remainder of his life. And after the final sentence he had an opportunity to escape which he rejected on the grounds that the laws of his city under which he had grown up should be, under any and every circumstance, strictly obeyed. He did not exactly seek martyrdom. That was not his style. But, again no doubt to the irritation of his enemies, he did nothing whatever to avoid it.

His many-sided and powerful personality, together with the deep affection and enormous literary and philosophical power of Plato, have made this simple, dignified and voluntary death indeed into a martyrdom. Among those who had accused and condemned him there must have been many honest and well-meaning citizens, and none of these could at the time have imagined that the effect of their action would be so strikingly opposite to anything which they had intended. For the future Socrates was to be the symbol of a loftier patriotism and a higher kind of morality than those of the city. Socrates was to be wholly exonerated from all the charges against him. Rather it was the city herself which could be reproached for not believing in the gods which Socrates worshipped and in failing to educate the youth along the lines laid down by him. His accusers had aimed merely at getting rid of an influence which had been proved to be disruptive. Posterity was only to see that they had put a good man to death, which was true, and for the most part was to subscribe to Socrates' own view that for an action unjust in itself there can be no possible justification.

The full effects of the Socratic revolution in thought and morality did not become immediately apparent, were certainly not imagined or intended by Socrates himself and were only dimly discernible even to Plato. They could not indeed be fully revealed until the political organisation of the city-state in which Socrates had thrived had been replaced by the wider and different organisations of the empire of Alexander and his successors. It is customary to say that neither Plato nor Aristotle, great political thinkers as they were, could ever advance to the idea of a really national or international state. It is extremely unlikely however that, even if they had been able to imagine these subsequent accumulations of individuals, they would have regarded them as an advance at all. Nor was this because of ignorance. They were perfectly well acquainted with the organisations of the great civilized states of Egypt and Persia and, along with all the Greeks, they believed that their own city-states were superior, with more to offer to their citizens and more brilliant achievements to their credit. The philosophers were ready enough to discuss what was the ideal size or the ideal constitution for these small units, but scarcely anyone imagined or maintained that they could be usefully replaced by something entirely different until this change had in fact taken place behind the backs, as it were, of the philosophers.

It is noteworthy that from Plato onwards hardly a single philosopher could be found who would advocate the kind of democracy which Pericles had extolled in his funeral speech. It might be admitted that tyranny was even worse than a thorough-going democracy, but nothing else was. And it was Socrates who, more than any other man, began the process of undermining the intellectual and moral structure on which the faith that Pericles held had rested. No doubt it sounded innocent and amusing enough to point out that, if you were suffering from a disease, you would be wiser to consult a doctor than a cobbler or maker of ropes. But when this argument was pressed further so as to show that in all matters of importance the only opinion worth having was that of an expert, one was already not far from admitting that in politics, which were certainly important, experts were also necessary. But what chance would an expert have of being heard in an Athenian Assembly dominated by a collection of cobblers, shipbuilders, tanners and all the rest who, while no doubt expert in their own trades, had never really thought of what politics was about except in so far as it affected their own interests? A good politician ought to know, in the first place, what was meant by a good city, just as a good cobbler knew what a good shoe ought to be. Socrates, to his own modest surprise, discovers that he is the only Athenian who has ever bothered seriously to consider this point. A number of politicians pretend to know and even think they do know, but, under examination, they will be found to think that the 'goodness' of a city consists in something like its wealth or its military power. And Socrates, though he admits he knows little enough, does at least know that such things in themselves have nothing to do with goodness. What makes a city good is the goodness of her citizens, the health of what he calls their 'souls'. And a soul can only become good by a process of continual self-examination; 'the unexamined life is not worth living'. Things being as they are, Socrates knew quite well that with these obviously true and obviously unusual views he would never get a hearing in the Assembly, and it would be a waste of time to try. He therefore takes the smallest possible part in politics, though he is always ready to fulfil every legal obligation asked of him by the state.

Readers of Plato's Socratic dialogues will, while admiring both the character and dexterity of Socrates himself, often be surprised to find that, though Socrates is expert in asking his opponents extremely awkward questions, none of these highly intelligent men seems capable of asking in return some questions which might embarrass him. What would he do, for example, if told by Athens to go and fight in an obviously unjust war? Or, is the war with Sparta a just war? Such questions as these are natural ones to anyone brought up to believe that there is truth in Socrates' doctrine of the

final and ultimate importance of justice and of the purity of individual morality. Surprising as it may seem to us, it is very likely that these questions never occurred to Socrates at all or to any of his fellow-citizens. With all his originality and all his idiosyncrasies he was utterly and entirely a man of the fifth century. To such a man there was nothing unusual in attempting to define justice or injustice, but no definition of justice was conceivable which could include the possibility of setting oneself above the laws of one's country.

He had grown to maturity in the Athens of Pericles, and whatever he may have thought of Pericles' precise political dispositions, it was this Athens and the friends he had had there which he loved. His love for her was so intense and his whole attitude so unlike that of a political revolutionary that it may never have crossed his mind that he was playing so large a part in the destruction of the whole basis on which Periclean Athens had stood. We have seen how for a short time there existed in this city a living harmony, reconciling and drawing strength from such tensions and oppositions as those between the old and the new, the one and the many, freedom and authority. The heroic virtues of the past were transforming and being transformed by the city of the present. The ideal Athenian was to combine the qualities of Achilles and of Odysseus; he was to have a sense of personal honour as keen as that of the hero of the *Iliad* and a versatility and capacity for endurance as great as those of the hero of the *Odyssey*. Yet both personal honour and individual versatility were to find their fulfilment in the city and in her great aim of glory in the present and for all time.

After Socrates this synthesis, this harmony, was to become impossible. It was to dissolve in two different directions. On the one hand those who most fervently believed in the primacy of the individual soul and its moral health would neglect politics altogether. If there was a community at all it would be a community of friendly philosophers. On the other hand those who still asserted that man was a political animal were no longer to believe that politics could be managed by the man in the street. The man in the street was ignorant and, if ignorant, likely to be harmful. He was to need the guidance and, if necessary, the compulsion of the expert. If Socrates himself were to be shown a medieval monastery on the one hand and a modern totalitarian state on the other and asked whether he preferred either of them to the Athens he had known, it is easy to imagine what his answer would be. But it is not easy to see how he would deal with the suggestion that the theoretical basis for each of these organisations may be found in his own thought. They indeed took long to mature and many different factors intervened, but something very like blueprints for both of them were developed quickly by Plato, his brilliant and devoted disciple.

Socrates is the last and greatest paradox of this great and paradoxical age. We may agree with his friends that he was the best, wisest, most patriotic and most god-fearing of men; but it is hard not to agree also with those who accused him of not believing in the gods in whom the city believed. He was to lead the way into a new age, an age of criticism and philosophy. But the age which he had loved had gone for ever except in so far as, like the Athenian dead whom Pericles praised, its 'glory

Greek fighting an Amazon. From a cuirass, fourth century

remains eternal in men's minds, always there on the right occasion to stir others to speech or action'. And, to crown all paradoxes, in all this Golden Age of humanism the figure which still stands before us four-square, more clear and distinct than any other, in the full glow of actuality, is that of the great affirmer, and the still greater denier, Socrates, the son of Sophroniscus, whose thought could, and did, lead in almost every direction except towards that of 'the great aim' outlined by Pericles.

Dedicatory relief of Athena

A SHORT BOOK LIST

C. M. Bowra, *The Greek Experience*, London, Mentor Books (The New English Library); New York, The World Publishing Company and Mentor Books (The New American Library), 1957

C. M. Bowra, *Periclean Athens*, London, Weidenfeld & Nicolson; New York, The Dial Press, 1971

J. H. Finley, *Thucydides*, University of Michigan Press, 1963

W. K. C. Guthrie, *A History of Greek Philosophy* Vol. 3, Cambridge University Press, 1969

W. Jaeger, *Paideia: The Ideals of Greek Culture*, 3 Vols., translated by G. Highet, Oxford University Press, 1939–44

H. D. F. Kitto, *The Greeks*, London and New York, Penguin Books (Pelican), 1951

H. D. F. Kitto, *Form and Meaning in Drama*, London and New York, Methuen, 1956

C. H. Whitman, *Sophocles: A Study of Heroic Humanism*, Harvard University Press, 1951

TRANSLATIONS

D. Grene and R. Lattimore (editors), *Complete Greek Tragedies*, 9 Vols., University of Chicago Press, 1959

B. B. Rogers, *The Comedies of Aristophanes*, 6 Vols., London, Bell, 1910–16

R. Warner, *Thucydides: History of the Peloponnesian War*, London and New York, Penguin Books, 1954

LIST OF ILLUSTRATIONS

and photographic acknowledgments

Page numbers set in **bold** denote a colour illustration. The source of the photograph used is given in *italics*.

THE FIFTH CENTURY

page 12 Snake, probably from archaic pediment shown on page 14. 580–70 B.C. Acropolis Museum, Athens. *Harissiadis (George Rainbird Archives)*

14 Proteus. 580–70 B.C. Acropolis Museum, Athens. *Harissiadis (George Rainbird Archives)*

15 Acropolis. *Alison Frantz (George Rainbird Archives)*

17 Vase. 520 B.C. British Museum, London. *Derrick Witty (George Rainbird Archives)*

18 Kore. 510 B.C. Acropolis Museum, Athens. *Harissiadis (George Rainbird Archives)*

21 Hera or Persephone. 480–70 B.C. *Staatliche Museen zu Berlin*

22 Aphrodite. Classical. *Courtesy of the Trustees of the British Museum, London*

AESCHYLUS: THE OLD AND THE NEW

24 Helmet. 460 B.C. *Courtesy of the Trustees of the British Museum, London*

27 Megakles the Fair. 500 B.C. Acropolis Museum, Athens. *Harissiadis (George Rainbird Archives)*

28–9 Relief from base of a statue. *c.* 510 B.C. National Museum, Athens. *Harissiadis (George Rainbird Archives)*

30 North frieze of the Siphnian Treasure House. *c.* 525 B.C. Delphi Museum. *Harissiadis (George Rainbird Archives)*

32 (left) Marble gravestone. *c.* 510 B.C. National Museum, Athens. *Mansell collection*
(above right) Vase. *c.* 450 B.C. Soprintendenza alle Antichità, Palermo. *Mansell collection*

32–3 Amphora. *c.* 525 B.C. Museo Gregoriano Etrusco, Rome. *Mansell collection*

34 (left) Vase. 520–10 B.C. *Courtesy of the Trustees of the British Museum, London*

page 34–5 North frieze of the Siphnian Treasure House. *c.* 525 B.C. Delphi Museum. *Harissiadis*

35 (right) Vase. 520–10 B.C. *Courtesy of the Trustees of the British Museum, London*

36 Kore. *c.* 510 B.C. Acropolis Museum, Athens. *Harissiadis (George Rainbird Archives)*

39 Bronze head. 490 B.C. National Museum, Athens. *Harissiadis (George Rainbird Archives)*

40 Remains of the Mycenaean Walls. *Harissiadis (George Rainbird Archives)*

43 Vase. *c.* 490 B.C. Vienna. *Mansell collection*

44 Tombstone. *c.* 510 B.C. National Museum, Athens. *Harissiadis (George Rainbird Archives)*

AESCHYLUS: FREEDOM AND AUTHORITY

46 Vase. *c.* 430 B.C. *Courtesy of the Trustees of the British Museum, London*

48 Drawing from a vase. East Berlin. *Mansell collection*

49 Vase. *c.* 370 B.C. Museo Nazionale, Naples. *Mansell collection*

51 Vase. *c.* 460 B.C. *Courtesy of the Trustees of the British Museum, London*

55 Vase. *c.* 425 B.C. *Ashmolean Museum, Oxford*

57 Marble horse. *c.* 500 B.C. Acropolis Museum, Athens. *Harissiadis (George Rainbird Archives)*

58 Blond Boy in marble. 480 B.C. Acropolis Museum, Athens. *Harissiadis (George Rainbird Archives)*

61 Terracotta relief. 470–60 B.C. Museo Nazionale, Taranto. *Soprintendenza alle Antichità della Puglia (George Rainbird Archives)*

62 (left) Vase. 440–30 B.C. *Courtesy of the Trustees of the British Museum, London* (right) Vase. Fifth-century. *Courtesy of the Trustees of the British Museum, London*

67 Bronze statuette. 450 B.C. National Museum, Athens. *Harissiadis (George Rainbird Archives)*

68–9 Areopagus. *Harissiadis (George Rainbird Archives)*

PERICLES: THE POWER AND THE GLORY

70 Pericles in marble. Roman copy of fifth-century Greek original. British Museum, London. *Derrick Witty (George Rainbird Archives)*

72 Frieze. –432 B.C. British Museum, London. *Derrick Witty (George Rainbird Archives)*

73 Themistocles. Roman copy from Greek original of *c.* 450 B.C. Museo Ostiense, Ostia. *Gabinetto Fotografico Nazionale, Rome*

74–5 'Lenormant' relief. *c.* 400 B.C. Acropolis Museum, Athens. *Harissiadis (George Rainbird Archives)*

77 Relief from Temple of Brauron. National Museum, Athens. *Harissiadis*

79 The Long Walls. *Harissiadis (George Rainbird Archives)*

80 Treasure House, Delphi. *Harissiadis (George Rainbird Archives)*

82 Lekythos. *c.* 440 B.C. *Courtesy of the Trustees of the British Museum, London*

83 Cup. *c.* 525 B.C. *Staatliche Museen zu Berlin*

THE GREAT AIM

page 88 Tombstone. *c.* 410 B.C. National Museum, Athens. *Harissiadis*

90 Tombstone. 470 B.C. *Courtesy of the Trustees of the British Museum, London*

92 Vase. *c.* 430 B.C. *Courtesy of the Trustees of the British Museum, London*

94 Vase. *c.* 470 B.C. National Museum, Athens. *George Rainbird Archives*

95 Vase. *c.* 425 B.C. *Ashmolean Museum, Oxford*

97 Detail of statue of Apollo from west pediment of Temple of Zeus at Olympia. *c.* 460 B.C. Olympia Museum. *Harissiadis*

98 Relief. *c.* 460 B.C. National Museum, Athens. *Harissiadis (George Rainbird Archives)*

100 (left) Cup. *c.* 500 B.C. *Courtesy of the Trustees of the British Museum, London*

100–1 Cup. *c.* 490 B.C. *Martin-von-Wagner Museum der Universitat, Würzburg (George Rainbird Archives)*

101 (right) Vase. *c.* 510 B.C. *Courtesy of the Trustees of the British Museum, London*

102 Jug. *c.* 430 B.C. Fletcher Fund, 1937, Metropolitan Museum of Art, New York. *Mansell collection*

103 Vase. 450–40 B.C. *Courtesy of the Trustees of the British Museum, London*

104–5 Relief. *c.* 510 B.C. National Museum, Athens. *Harissiadis (George Rainbird Archives)*

107 Vase. Fifth-century. *Courtesy of the Trustees of the British Museum, London*

BUILDING OF THE PARTHENON

109 Pentelicon marble. *Harissiadis*

110 Agora Museum, *American School of Classical Studies at Athens*

113 Parthenon. *Harissiadis*

115 Parthenon. *Harissiadis*

116 Frieze. –432 B.C. Acropolis Museum, Athens. *Harissiadis*

118 Frieze. –432 B.C. Acropolis Museum, Athens. *Harissiadis (George Rainbird Archives)*

119 Parthenon. *Alison Frantz (George Rainbird Archives)*

120–1 Frieze. –432 B.C. *Courtesy of the Trustees of the British Museum, London*

123 Frieze. –432 B.C. *Courtesy of the Trustees of the British Museum, London*

125 Frieze. –432 B.C. Acropolis Museum, Athens. *Harissiadis (George Rainbird Archives)*

126–7 Erechtheum, Acropolis. *Harissiadis*

128 Detail of bronze statue. *c.* 455 B.C. National Museum, Athens, *Harissiadis*

131 From the east pediment. –432 B.C. British Museum, London. *Derrick Witty (George Rainbird Archives)*

SOPHOCLES

132 Bronze head. Roman copy of Greek original. *Courtesy of the Trustees of the British Museum, London*

136 Statuette of Athena. Roman copy from Greek original of 438 B.C. National Museum, Athens. *Harissiadis (George Rainbird Archives)*

page **137** Varvakion statuette of Athena 3 foot 5 inches (1·045 metres) high. Roman copy 130 A.D. from Greek original of 438 B.C. National Museum, Athens. *Harissiadis (George Rainbird Archives)*

138 Roman copy of shield of Athena Parthenos of 438 B.C. British Museum, London. *Derrick Witty (George Rainbird Archives)*

140 Relief. *c.* 460 B.C. Museo Nazionale, Rome. *Mansell collection*

143 Bronze statue. *c.* 475 B.C. Delphi Museum. *Alison Frantz (George Rainbird Archives)*

145 Coin. Roman copy 133 A.D. from Greek original of *c.* 430 B.C. Museo Archeologico, Florence. *Soprintendenza alle Antichità dell'Etruria*

147 Knucklebone vase. 460 B.C. *Courtesy of the Trustees of the British Museum, London*

148–9 Temple of Poseidon. *Harissiadis*

SOPHOCLES: HIS LAST PLAY

150 Delphi. *Harissiadis (George Rainbird Archives)*

152 Vase. 460 B.C. Musée du Louvre, Paris. *Mansell collection*

153 Vase. 440–30 B.C. *Courtesy of the Trustees of the British Museum, London*

155 From the east pediment of the Temple of Zeus at Olympia. *c.* 460 B.C. *Hirmer Fotoarchiv, Munich*

159 Vase. *c.* 440 B.C. British Museum, London. *Derrick Witty (George Rainbird Archives)*

160 Bronze statue. *c.* 475 B.C. Delphi Museum. *Harissiadis (George Rainbird Archives)*

162 Vase. Late fifth-century. *Courtesy of the Trustees of the British Museum, London*

164 Vase. *c.* 480 B.C. *Courtesy of the Trustees of the British Museum, London*

167 Head of Hera. 420 B.C. National Museum, Athens. *Harissiadis (George Rainbird Archives)*

EURIPIDES AND INSECURITY

170 Vase. Fifth-century. Musée du Louvre, Paris. *Maurice Chuzeville Photographe*

172 Vase. 480–70 B.C. *Courtesy of the Trustees of the British Museum, London*

172–3 Vase. *c.* 420 B.C. Museo Etrusco Gregoriano, Vatican. *Mansell collection*

178–9 Two vases. 500–490 B.C. Munich. *Mansell collection*

180 Vase. 480–70 B.C. *Courtesy of the Trustees of the British Museum, London*

181 Statuette. *c.* 450 B.C. *Mansell collection*

185 Vase. Late fifth-century. National Museum, Athens. *Harissiadis (George Rainbird Archives)*

186–7 Gravestone. *c.* 500 B.C. National Museum, Athens. *Harissiadis (George Rainbird Archives)*

188 Vase. 380 B.C. British Museum, London. *Derrick Witty (George Rainbird Archives)*

190–1 Relief. *c.* 400 B.C. National Museum, Athens. *Harissiadis (George Rainbird Archives)*

page 192 Drinking jar. *c.* 400 B.C. *Courtesy of the Trustees of the British Museum, London*

193 Vase. 400–390 B.C. *Courtesy of the Trustees of the British Museum, London*

195 Relief. Roman copy carved 100 A.D. Figures derived from prototypes from fourth-century Greece. British Museum, London. *Mansell collection*

197 Temple of Athena Nike, finished 524(?) B.C. *Harissiadis (George Rainbird Archives)*

THUCYDIDES: LAW AND NATURE

198 Theatre of Dionysus, Athens. *Harissiadis*

200 Marble bust. Second-century A.D. copy. Agora Museum, American School of Classical Studies at Athens. *Harissiadis (George Rainbird Archives)*

204–5 The Pnyx. *Harissiadis*

210 (left) Kleroterion. *c.* 450 B.C. Agora Museum, American School of Classical Studies at Athens. *Harissiadis (George Rainbird Archives)*
(right) Bronze tickets. *c.* 460 B.C. British Museum, London. *Mansell collection*

211 (left) Jurors' ballots. Agora Museum, American School of Classical Studies at Athens. *Harissiadis (George Rainbird Archives)*
(right) Replicas of fifth-century waterpots. Agora Museum, American School of Classical Studies at Athens. *Mansell collection*

215 Relief. *c.* 410 B.C. Acropolis Museum, Athens. *Harissiadis (George Rainbird Archives)*

216 Lekythos. 420–400 B.C. British Museum, London. *Derrick Witty (George Rainbird Archives)*

ARISTOPHANES: WAR AND PEACE

218 Statuettes from Athenian graves. Fourth-century B.C. Rogers Fund, 1913, *Metropolitan Museum of Art, New York*

224–5 Theatre of Epidaurus. *c.* 430 B.C. *Harissiadis*

230 Statuettes from Athenian graves. Fourth-century B.C. Rogers Fund, 1913, *Metropolitan Museum of Art, New York*

233 Figures. 340–30 B.C. British Museum, London. *Mansell collection*

SOCRATES: THE END AND THE BEGINNING

234 Roman copy of Greek fourth-century B.C. statuette. *Courtesy of the Trustees of the British Museum, London*

236 Miniature reliefs. Fourth-century B.C. *Mansell collection*

241 Relief. *c.* 400 B.C. National Museum, Athens. *Harissiadis (George Rainbird Archives)*

244 Relief. *c.* 400 B.C. National Museum, Athens. *Harissiadis*

248 Relief. Fourth-century B.C. *Courtesy of the Trustees of the British Museum, London*

250 Relief. 400 B.C. Acropolis Museum, Athens. *Harissiadis (George Rainbird Archives)*

INDEX

Figures in **bold type** refer to colour plates; those in *italics* to black-and-white illustrations.

Acharnians, 228–9
Achilles, *32*
Acropolis, *15*, **79**; 16, 25, 71, 76, 112
Aeschylus, 26, 34, 37; in Aristophanes'
    Frogs, 34–5; innovations in drama, 38;
    comparison with Shakespeare, 38, 41, 42;
    comparison with Sophocles and Euri-
    pides, 42, 45, 144–5, 151; trilogies of, 45;
    view of gods, 48, 50, 189; concern with
    politics, 50, 66; death 194. See also under
    *Agamemnon, Eumenides, Libation Bearers,
    Oresteia, Prometheia, Prometheus Bound,
    Suppliants*
Agamemnon, *46*
Agamemnon, 45, 49, 59, 64
Agariste, 71
agôn, 220, 221, 232
aitios, 168
Ajax, *32*
Ajax, 151, 153
Alcibiades, 26, 87, 243, 245
Alcmaeonidae, 37, 71
Anaxagoras, 117, 122, 192, 246
Antigone, 152, 153, 161
Aphrodite, 22, **98**(?), *140–1*(?)
Apollo, **30**, **97**, *118*; 124
Areopagus, **68–9**
Ares, *34*
Ariadne, *193*

Aristides, 71, 76, 122
Aristogiton, 37
aristoi, 26
Aristophanes, 33–5, 37; treatment of Euri-
    pides, 182–3, 194, 233, 235–6; assessment
    of, 219; attacks on political figures, 223,
    226–8; pacifism of, 228–32; treatment of
    Socrates, 235–6. See also under *Acharn-
    ians, Birds, Frogs, Knights, Lysistrata,
    Peace*
Aristotle, 102, 133, 200, 240, 246–7
Artemis, **30**, **116**, *118*
Athena, *51*, *250*
Athena Parthenos, *136*, **137**; 124, 129, 142
Athena Nike, temple of, *110*, **197**, **215**
Athenians, as innovators, 13, 25; Corinthian
    opinion of, 14; place of poets among, 33
Athens, in 5th century B.C., 13; 'the tyrant
    city', 20; pro-Spartan party in, 25–6;
    citizen army of, 31; and Sparta, 31, 93;
    dramatic contests in, 37, 38; drama of, 38,
    41–2; negotiations with Sparta, 71–2, 76;
    rebuilds walls, 76; navy of, 76; helps
    Sparta, 78; expansion abroad, 78; plague,
    81; imperial power, 84; constitution of,
    91; architecture of, 91, 109; freedom of
    speech at, 222

Bacchae, 180, 183, 189, 192, 194, 223

Basile, **186–7**
Birds, 231
Brasidas, 230
Byzantine churches in Athens, 16, 19
Byzantium, Greek Empire of, 19

Callicrates, 114
Caryatids (at the Erechtheum), **126–7**
Charmides, 237
Cimon, 26, 66, 76, 78, 109, 111, 206
Cleisthenes, 37, 71, 243
Cleon, 84, 85, 206, 212–15, 226, 227, 230
comedy, old, 42, 196, 220–2, 223
Crassus, 194
Cratinus, 114
Critias, 118, 237, 243, 245

daimonion, 240
Damon, 117
Delos, Confederacy of, 71, 78
Delphi, oracle at, **150**; Treasure House at, **80**
Demosthenes, 227
Diodotus, 212–15
Dionysia, festival of the, 37, 38, 220
Dionysus, *181, 185, 190–1, 193*; 119, 183, 189
Dionysus, theatre of, *198*
dithyramb, 38

Echelos, *186*
Eleusis, sanctuary at, 112
Epicharmus of Syracuse, 220
Epidaurus, theatre at, *224*
Erechtheum, the, *110*, **126–7**; 38, 114, 130
Erinyes, the, *49*
Eros, *193*
Eumenides, 122
Eunomia, 31
Euripides, in Aristophanes' *Frogs*, 34, 35, 66; plays of, 42, 45, 134; comparison with Sophocles, 142, 151, 169, 180, 181, 183; attitude towards the gods, 144–5, 169,

177, 180–2, 183–4, 189; love of Athens, 158, 161, 171, 172, 173–4; patriotism of, 177; realism of, 182–3; comparison with Aeschylus, 180, 181, 183, 189; admired by Socrates, 192; death of, 194; reputation, 194; later plays of, 195, 223. See also under *Bacchae, Helen, Heracles, Hippolytus, Ion, Medea*
Euripides the Athenian (by George Seferis), 171, 176, 192, 194

Frogs, 33–5, 119, 151, 221

Gorgias of Leontini, 122, 238
Greek language, 14, 16

hamartia, 133
Harmodius, 37
Hegeso, *244*
Helen, 134, 182, 189
Hephaistos, temple of, 112
Hera, *21(?), 167*
Heracles, 171
Heraclitus, 31
Hermae, mutilation of the, 25, 231, 243
Hermes, *34, 186–7*
Herodotus, *200(?)*; 62, 200–2
Hippias, 37
Hippocratic school of medicine, 202
Hippolytus, 177, 180–2, 189
Homer, 48, 66, 129, 142, 174–5. See also under *Iliad, Odyssey.*

Ictinus, 114
Iliad, 31, 66, 129, 174, 175
Ion, 177, 180

Kaloskagathos, 135
Knights, 227

Lenaea, festival of the, 220
Libation Bearers, 45
lipotaxia, 31

Lycurgus, 31
Lysistrata, 231–2

Marathon, battle of, 37
Medea, *170, 172*
Medea, 158, 172–4, 182, 184
Melos, subjugation of, 207, 208, 209
Menander, 196
Mnesicles, 114
Mycale, battle of, 71
Mytilene, revolt of, 210–11

Nicias, 25, 176, 209, 217, 227; Peace of, 229–230
nomos, 199

Odeum, 112, 114
Odysseus, *43*
Odyssey, 174, 175
Oedipus, *152, 153, 162*
Oedipus at Colonus, 134, 142, 151, 153, 154, 156–8, 161–5, 171, 175; and Milton's *Samson Agonistes*, 165–6, 169
Oedipus Tyrannus, 45, 134, 153, 154, 217
Oresteia, 35, 45, 49–50, 52, 64, 65, 134
Orestes, *48*

Panathenaea, festival of the, 37, 114
parabasis, 220–1
parrhesia, 222
Parthenon, the, **40**, *110, 113,* **115**, *119, 131*; 13, 16, 38, 158; building of, 109, 112, 114, 117; architects of, 114; friezes of, **116**, *118, 120–1, 123,* **125**; 122, 124, 129, 142, 161; sculpture of, 129
Peace, 229–31
Peisistratus, 37, 38
Pericles, **70**, *72,* **138**; 'the age of', 13; love of Athens, 13, 14, 78, 91, 93–4, 96, 106–7; his building programme, 16, 109, 111–12; theory of democracy, 20, 71, 78, 87; comes to power, 25–6; holds law sacred, 31; concepts of honour and dishonour, 66, 84; imperial policy, 78, 81, 83–5; as recorded by Thucydides, 86; funeral speech of, 84, 89–91, 93–4, 96, 99–100; his 'great aim', 84, 85, 106–7; compares Sparta with Athens, 91, 93–4, 100–1; personal attacks on, 114, 117; represented by Phidias, 122; in comparison with Cleon, 84–5, 212–13; belief in freedom of speech, 239
Persians, 34–5, 226
Phidias, **138**; 19, 114, 117, 122, 124, 129, 130, 131, 133, 142
Philoctetes, 134, 153, 175
physis, 199, 202
Pindar, 122
Plataea, battle of, 71, 214, 217
Plato, *236*; his political ideal, 20, 200; contempt of democracy, 20, 87; appeal of Spartan system, 100; predilection for the city-state, 102–3, 246–7; on art, 130; on Socrates, 236–8, 240, 242, 246
pleonexia, 52
Poseidon, *118,* **128**
Poseidon, Temple of, at Sounium, **148–9**

Salamis, battle of, 37, 71
Socrates, *234, 236*; 31, 35, 199; view of gods, 122; admiration for Euripides, 192; as portrayed by Aristophanes, 235–6; by Plato, 236–7, 240; by Xenophon, 237, 238, 240; as distinct from sophists, 238; opposed by Periclean thought, 239, 247, 249; innovations in philosophy, 240, 242; trial of, 243, 246; death of, 246
sophists, 238, 240
Sophocles, *132*; 26, 38, 42, 45, 133; various interpretations of his plays, 135, 139; heroes of, 135, 139, 140; and Shakespeare, 144, 145–6; view of the gods, 144–5, 189, 207; personal life, 145–6, 151; qualities in his plays, 151, 152–3; love of Athens, 158, 161, 171. See also under *Ajax, Antigone, Oedipus at Colonus, Oedipus*

Tyrannus, Philoctetes, Women of Trachis.

Sparta, 20; Athenian admiration for, 25–6; citizen army of, 31; system of rule, 31; opposes Athens, 71, 72, 76; earthquake at, 78; discipline of, 91, 93

Sounium, Temple of Poseidon at, **148–9**

Suppliants, 62

Tacitus, 20

Themistocles, *73*; 20, 26, 38, 76, 78

Thrasymachus, 238

Thucydides, judgment on Pericles, 20; on tyrants, 37; on Themistocles, 76; hatred of Cleon, 84, 206; admiration for Pericles, 84, 85, 86–7, 106, 206; records Pericles' speeches, 86, 89; on democracy, 87; reticent about Athens' great buildings, 109; describes Athens' defeat in Sicily, 176; attitude towards war, 184, 202; pride in accuracy, 200; aim of his *History*, 200, 201; view of the gods, 202, 207, 209; account of the plague of Athens, 202, 204–5; on the revolution in Corcyra, 205–6; view of history, 206, 207, 209–10; use of irony, 207, 208; debate on fate of Mytilene, 210–14; account of battle of Plataea, 214, 217

Thucydides, son of Melesias, 109, 111, 206

thumos, 182

tragedies, Greek, 134

tyrants, of Athens, 37, 38; the Thirty, 117, 245

Women of Trachis, 134, 139, 142, 153

Xanthippus, 71, 76

Xenophon, 20, 100, 237, 238, 240

Zeus, **67**

Zeus of Artemisium, 124, 142

Zeus at Olympia, *145*; 124, 142